THE RISE OF THE CRAFT BRAND

THE RISE

OF THE

CRAFT BRAND

Why Small IS GOING TO BE
HUGE

BEN
ZIFKIN

FOUNDER & CEO OF HUBBA

THE RISE OF THE CRAFT BRAND

Why Small Is Going to Be Huge

ISBN   978-1-61961-431-4   *Paperback*

      978-1-61961-432-1   *Ebook*

For S, J and L...with love.

CONTENTS

———

ACKNOWLEDGMENTS

———

INSPIRED BY
My family at home
My family abroad
My family at work
And the Hubba community

INTRODUCTION

———

ONE WORD: HUMIDIFIERS

It was interesting to end up in the tech field despite not really touching a computer until my second year of university. In fact, I was on my way to law school when I sat down with my father, a lawyer, and showed him proposals for retail customers I drafted with the programming skills I had learned.

He said, "Why are you going to law school? You should do this."

So I did.

My first real job was with a technology start-up in 2001, where I joined early and the company grew to four hundred employees before the world imploded and the dot-com era came to an end. The second start-up I joined had me implementing enterprise software for huge organizations.

Although the software was revolutionary, in many cases, we just made bad processes go faster. This gave me the confidence to start my own company with a colleague in 2004. We focused on building an organization that worked with senior-level management of Fortune 1000 companies to make their businesses better through technology, primarily focusing on people and operations.

When I started my first business with my cofounder, I was twenty-seven. The company grew to well over 120 people in a couple of years and was acquired four years after its founding. The CEO of the acquiring company asked me to start and run international operations for his company, given my experiences living and working abroad.

I relocated to London, where I found myself removed from the familiar products that had surrounded me in my native Canada. I was even separated from my beloved Blackberry, to which I had been a devout user for years and years until a UK-based telephone company told me it wasn't compatible with their plans. I switched to an iPhone just as the device was newly released. All of a sudden, I possessed a better Internet connection and a superior browser and screen, but I was frustrated that I still couldn't find the information I was looking for.

I have to admit: I am a complete information junkie. I need

to know how things are made, where things are made, what things are made of, how things function, and where things go. It doesn't matter what it is—I just need to know about it. Given my technical background, I knew that the data that I wanted was out there somewhere. The technology was now readily available to bring me the answers, and I *wanted* the answers, except it quickly became evident that all of those pieces had yet to be put together.

Although the United States was heading into a recession in 2008, e-commerce sales were steadily increasing. Still, there remained a game of broken telephone, with companies, retailers, and merchants unable to convey digital information to the customer and consumers unable to find the details and stories about a particular product. Lost sales and frustrated customers represented a significant opportunity cost, and this was only going to become a bigger issue as the Internet and mobile adoption grew. My curiosity led me right into a massive void in the commerce ecosystem: there was no single, underlying commerce data company empowering the spread of information.

Today, only 25 percent of what you see online is correct. Seventy-five percent of product information is either incomplete or incorrect. Missing images, incomplete descriptions, inaccurate ingredients, wrong nutrition information, false claims, and old packaging photos are just a few of the issues that consumers encounter when they research and/or shop online. Knowing this, I pulled together some of the best technology minds, and we set out to correct it by building a monster commerce data company—*the* monster commerce data company. We also knew, given the inaccuracy of information, that we couldn't simply source content from the web, as combing through millions of web pages would not only be inefficient but also yield mainly flawed data. Nor could we depend on user-generated content, which could be inaccurate and inconsistent. There seemed to be only one solution: figuring out how to get the information from the brands themselves.

It turns out, brands were waiting for something like this. Retailers inundate marketers for brands with requests for pictures for an e-commerce site, descriptions for a flyer, and training materials for a staff. One retailer needs images or information in one format and another retailer needs it in a different format. Brands may have hundreds, even thousands of channels that need to be kept up-to-date, and all of the required information might sit in seventeen different internal systems, or on one spreadsheet hidden away on an employee's computer—either way, the status quo was ineffective, with information not getting to the people who needed it most, and it was potentially incorrect by the time it was filtered through so many channels.

Our goal was to build a platform for brands so they could manage their information from a single source and easily publish or share—in real-time—their most current, comprehensive, and consistent product information. We asked brands to contemplate one simple, yet critical question: If consumers are in the store aisle or on a browser evaluating your product versus a competitor's, what do you as a brand want to tell consumers at that moment to help them choose your product? Sadly, as things stand today, most of that information that the brand wants to articulate never reaches consumers at the moment they're making a purchasing decision. Hubba set out to change that—to empower consumers and allow brands to communicate easily with their audience.

I founded Hubba as an extension of my love for going after huge, tier-one companies, and I didn't know at the time that I had developed a bit of a blind spot. At first, we only went after the large companies. I had spent the last fifteen years of my career helping massive organizations figure out how to become better through the use of technology, and I loved working with global enterprises. We'd be in the midst of convincing multinationals such as Johnson & Johnson that we were a better option than bigger incumbent software companies, so I mostly brushed off requests from individual brand managers—requests like, "Help me manage the eighty e-mails and panicked phone calls I get each day from retailers and e-commerce sites asking for product images and descriptions."

After a few months of being in the market with our new platform, our chief business development officer took me aside, sat me down, and said, "It's cool you want to focus on 'big-game hunting' with larger enterprise deals, but you're not listening to the front-line, assistant brand manager out there, who's saying, 'Just make my life better.'"

I haven't stopped thanking him ever since.

We began to shift Hubba's focus from large companies to helping individuals who work in companies of all sizes. Instead of developing our business just through top-down enterprise deals, we went grassroots, launching the Hubba network in 2014. In the first four months, we brought on one thousand companies. Clearly, we were onto something. Something big. We now bring a thousand companies onto our system every few days.

When Hubba was just starting out, no one knew about us. We decided to change this by inviting ourselves to an important industry conference. Gartner, one of the world's most influential technology research firms, was hosting their 2013 Master Data Management Summit in Texas, where IT folks, data analysts, and the like were invited to focus on MDM—the discipline of getting all the customer information to one spot properly, or all of your company's product information to one spot properly, so there's a single source of information. It was very old-school technology, and the conference was pretty boring—all about data governance and such.

It was clear to us that we wanted Hubba to be the exact opposite of that. Although we were, in some respects, providing a similar service, we wanted our offering to be easy and cool to use, primarily for marketers, and with no implementation necessary. Simply log in and, if you know how to use Facebook, you'll know how to use Hubba.

As a small company back in 2013, we didn't have enough of a budget to pay to attend the conference, let alone exhibit alongside all of the old, legacy incumbents at the show. So we did what any self-respecting and ambitious start-up would do: we crashed it. Our team printed up a bunch of pamphlets titled, "We wanted to be the first to welcome you to Data Management 2004." The date was an intentional typo, calling out how antiquated these MDM methods really were. And at the bottom, it said, "If you would like to see how you can manage your data in 2013, please check us out."

We didn't take into account that the conference hotel

would be huge and that there was no way of knowing which rooms belonged to the hundreds of conference-goers versus those who belonged to other guests. As luck would have it, at 3:00 a.m., the conference organizers went around to each conference attendee's room and hung a welcome bag on the doorknob. So, at 3:30 a.m., our head of marketing snuck out of her room and trolled the halls, putting our pamphlet under each of those doors.

We listed our website so people could find us, and although we weren't even registered with the conference and didn't pay to attend, the conference's Twitter feed was filled with Hubba the next day. We received sign-ups on our platform from almost every single type of constituent that was there. We hijacked the conference by telling people, "Listen, all these dinosaurs from ten years ago aren't actually helping you manage things. If you want to know how to do it now, check us out."

We were saying much more than just, "We're better." We were saying that we get it, you've been using these systems for years, they don't address the new world of commerce, and now it's time for something new. Hubba was that something new, and we were gaining traction using the same strategies outlined in this book. We were scrappy. It is amazing how, for the simple price of a plane ticket—a fraction of the cost that major players were paying to attend—we were able to drive the conversation of the conference. This was our version of "poking the bear," something I'll touch on again in Chapter 5 when relating stories of Dollar Shave Club and Hampton Creek.

We wanted to be the first to welcome you to

Data Management 2004

(If you would like to see how you can manage your data in **2013**, please check us out.)

www.hubba.com/TheNewWay

 hubba

Still, I admit, it was hard for me to turn my focus away from the big brands. As Hubba's user base grew, I noticed numerous smaller brands cropping up, and instead of just needing to share product information with existing partners, they wanted to know how we could help them get discovered by other retailers to grow their businesses.

I initially brushed off those requests. Having focused on large companies my entire professional life, I wanted to build what I thought was a "proper" firm that could compete with massive software companies such as SAP, Oracle, and Informatica from day one. As a start-up, I wanted to be able to walk into Proctor & Gamble or Unilever and not be laughed out of the room. As I mentioned, working with the small and medium business (SMB) segment was not my initial focus, having grown up in a world where you want big-name logos as your customers from the very beginning. I feared working with SMBs would be an indication that we couldn't make it with the big guys and could potentially limit our market.

An interesting company called Crane Humidifiers changed all that.

I was asked to speak at Internet Retailer Conference in Chicago at the beginning of 2015. A Chicago-based company, Crane Humidifiers, had been pretty vocal about how Hubba could benefit them if we focused on a few specific things, so I asked Joe, my contact there, if we could meet at the conference and walk the floor together. I wanted to see what his world looked like now that I was thinking about smaller brands.

Crane Humidifiers was founded in 2005, "on the belief that design is an attitude and the home is a personal expression of an individual's lifestyle." They state that "while humidifiers, air purifiers, and space heaters are some of the best ways to control indoor air pollutants and heating, most people don't break into a smile about these traditionally unexciting humidity, air quality, and heating solutions."

As we strolled up and down the conference aisles, I listened carefully to Joe. When he spoke, it was clear he was passionate about humidifiers, and that Crane envisioned them not as utilitarian household items, but nicely designed and beautiful. The humidifiers were not just physically beneficial but also emotionally rewarding. It threw me for a massive loop. Of all things, humidifiers. But Joe's passion was contagious. As we walked the show floor, I realized that Joe woke up every day with a real mission in his life: to change how products are designed in an attempt toward better living.

There is no doubt that Crane is changing the face of humidifiers, as each product is radically different from the traditional, utilitarian, boxy machines I originally associated with the appliance. Instead, Crane produced teardrop-shaped humidifiers, duck- and tiger- and frog-shaped humidifiers, and air purifiers made to look like penguins.

I already had a humidifier at home, but after Joe inspired

me, I promptly bought another one—not because I needed it, but because I believed in it. I wanted to be part of what Crane was doing, and instead of choosing any old humidifier off Amazon, I decided to support Crane with a purchase, thereby becoming part of a community of people who were passionate about their humidifiers.

That humidifiers could be cool to me was strange, and it proved Crane was on to something. I started to consider other craft brands I came across in a new light, no longer brushing them aside. What I discovered was an overflow of passion and involvement. Whether it was a holistic cosmetics company, organic cotton baby toys, or protein bars, they each possessed unbelievable, unique stories and sought to share them with the world. Passion was one of their many commonalities. Across the board, I saw companies with scarce resources and small staffs taking advantage of new distribution models to sell innovative products driven by a mission or a unique story. It was just a matter of getting their stories out in a complete, consistent, engaging, and timely manner.

A lot of the craft brands I encountered were new, but some of them were companies started a century ago—sometimes by someone's grandfather and then later resuscitated by a relative. Usually, there was an emotional component triggering the start of the brand—sometimes it was a passion project, a student's pet project, an unemployed job seeker's side gig, an investment banker's renouncement of the old world, or someone who just realized the world was missing something they could provide. Whatever the reason, it came with a story.

Generally, craft brands weren't offering cheaper prices. Instead, they focused on carefully producing items on a smaller scale, such as craft foods or craft baby toys. It wasn't the products themselves that mattered as much as the methods with which they were produced, or the mission behind them, and this includes everything from humidifiers to butter to razors to dog shampoo.

For instance, today most people know Under Armour as a massive sports apparel company. Before they became a household name, they were a craft brand. Although they didn't have the huge marketing budgets of their competitors, they manufactured high-quality cotton hoodies that were also waterproof. World of Angus started a vibrant online community by selling luxury dog shampoo direct to consumers online. Stirling Creamery created butter using quality ingredients and artisanal practices. Dapple Baby provided nontoxic cleaning solutions for people with kids and toddlers.

There is no disputing that the commerce landscape

has permanently changed and continues to do evolve. Retailers held the power for decades; they were the ones who knew and owned the consumer, and brands were beholden to them to get a product out to the world. Now, structural changes to the ways consumers buy and sell are bringing more and more craft brands to prominence. Technology has allowed e-commerce sites to pop up and brands to sell direct to consumers. The book will explore how decentralization of commerce, increased awareness of consumers, and the rise of the craft brand will lead to massive changes in market share in every industry.

The pendulum of power is swinging from retailers to brands, representing a huge change. If we understand how, by studying examples of successful craft brands challenging the market shares of large corporations and the structural forces behind this, we can be better prepared to take advantage of the shift.

This is more than an evolution—a whole new species of commerce has been created. By 2017, approximately one in four purchases will be made online. Almost all transactions—online or in-store—are researched beforehand and influenced by digital product information. As people do more things digitally—buying online as opposed to going to a store and picking up something physical with their hands—the stories behind a product, and getting those stories out there, will make a huge difference in whether a brand succeeds or fails. It no longer comes down to how two products look side by side on a shelf, but how well a mission and vision are communicated through a screen. Consumers are hungrier for information than ever before, with increased access online and through mobile to empower each buying decision. It is not only important, but imperative that small brands have a way to convey their stories in order to further their growth and that big companies don't underestimate emerging challengers or the power of a story.

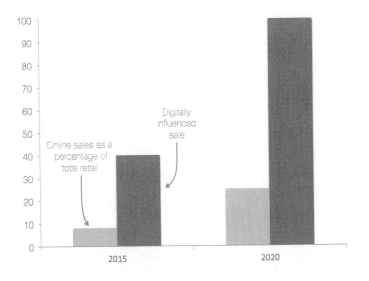

PART I

—

THE END OF BIG

THE NEW WORLD
OF COMMERCE

—

Until recently, commerce was unchanged for decades, if not centuries. If you needed something, you walked, rode your horse, biked, or drove to a store, picked out the product, paid for it, and brought it home. For brands, the main way to get a product into the hands of the consumer was through a retailer—or a distributor, who would handle getting it to a retailer.

Historically, retailers owned the consumer relationship. Retailers chose what brands to carry, where and how to feature their products, and ultimately decided what reached the consumer and when. The power to get products distributed and sold was held in the hands of a select few, and brands had to fight for attention. The amount of shelf space was finite. Buyers cared about keeping shelves stocked, not necessarily finding the latest and greatest new thing, or taking risks with new products. Massive Consumer Packaged Goods (CPG) companies—large players with big marketing, promotion, and comp budgets—dominated the retail world and its shelves. Reaching consumers meant brands had to overcome many obstacles and gatekeepers.

For one, the old world relied on brands wining and dining retail buyers, literally. The practice of excessive entertainment budgets for wining and dining continued until retailers implemented policies to put an end to it. It then morphed into creative and figurative ways to entice retail buyers to carry specific products. As early as the early 1900s, CPG companies entrenched themselves with retailers. Toward the end of the century, as regulations and policies changed, the way to reach consumers was to get your brand in front of them, via print, radio, or television. Smaller brands lacked funds to pay for airtime that could compete with larger companies, and consumer education was restricted to advertisement—which was often riddled with blurred truths. Avenues for discovering new brands and products were limited, leading to tunnel vision around products and their usage.

Commerce was cyclical and unchanging: the company with the most ads and distribution deals reached consumers, and their perpetual growth lead to yet more ads and more shelf space. For decades, big brands reigned.

All of that has changed and continues to shift. The rise of technology lifted massive barriers to entry faced by small brands attempting to reach consumers. We now live in a decentralized and, in many ways, more democratized world of commerce. While retailers continue to hold a great deal of influence, they no longer hold all of the power. Consumers have changed as well, as have habits of consumption—more specifically, the methods by which we all learn about and buy products. In addition, massive shifts in market share are occurring, with the little guys—with their leaner staffs and smaller budgets—challenging large corporations. The wave created by all these forces is now cresting.

After Jill Abramson was ousted as executive editor of the *New York Times* in 2014, the newspaper's own rigorous self-examination of its strategies was released. The report on innovation acknowledged that competitors like *Huffington Post* had surpassed the *Times* in reader traffic years before, and Buzzfeed pulled ahead in 2013. *Times'* home page visitor traffic peaked in 2011 at 160 million and quickly dropped in half (or free fell, depending on who you ask) to 80 million in 2013. The following graph of visitor traffic appeared to corroborate the feeling in the media world that its leading publication had nose-dived into oblivion.

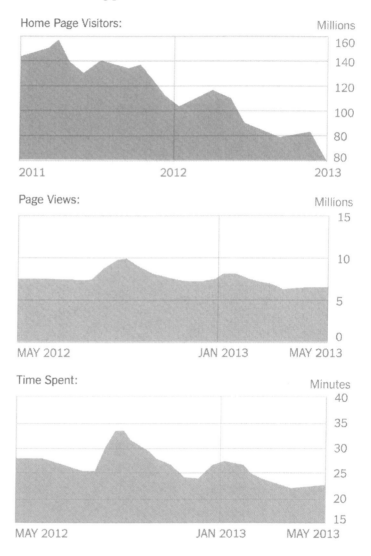

Home Page Visitors: — Millions

160
140
120
100
80
80

2011   2012   2013

Page Views: — Millions

15
10
5
0

MAY 2012   JAN 2013   MAY 2013

Time Spent: — Minutes

40
35
30
25
20
15

MAY 2012   JAN 2013   MAY 2013

Yet when digging deeper into what was going on, it was very intriguing to note that total page views of articles during that same period held steady, as did the average time spent on the site.

This data confirmed that people were still reading the *Times'* content in the same quantity, yet they did not necessarily go to the newspaper's home page to reach it. Media accessibility had been decentralized, and online readers still accessed the *Times* online content, but a growing number were doing it through other means.

What happened in the media world is a perfect analogy for what is now happening in commerce, and it is a perfect example of decentralization. One used to have to go to the *Times's* home page to read their articles, but increasingly, readers were able to access articles of interest through Facebook, Twitter, Pinterest, LinkedIn, e-mail, and more. Instead of having to go to a destination to find the content, the content comes to you. In much the same way, consumers used to have to go to a brick-and-mortar retail store to buy a product. You had to go somewhere to complete a transaction. Even Amazon was a destination and represented the beginning of this whole new world opening up, whereas now the transaction comes to you.

There exists a vast middle ground—unclaimed land where

brands can reach consumers. For one, there are direct-to-consumer sales, usually through online platforms like Shopify. Brands have access to audiences through social media; for example, the "buy" button on Facebook. If a friend "likes" an item on Facebook, and if a company lists it there, you can buy it, even without having to leave the social media platform. The same goes for Pinterest buy buttons—users are no longer relegated to "liking" or "pinning" products, as they now have the option to purchase items.

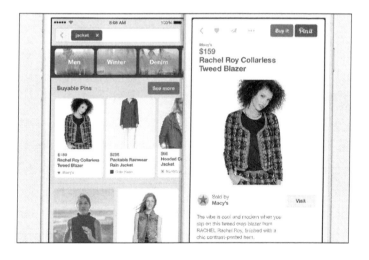

Both are perfect examples of our decentralized world of commerce—illustrating how you no longer have to head to a destination to buy a product. While fewer people do visit the retail store channel, brands' sales can remain steady and even expand through other channels and means.

For the most part, consumers used to be creatures of habit and shop mainly at one or two of their favorite stores for a product. Now they can wind up anywhere. There are countless channels; for example, eBay marketplaces allow vendors and brands alike to sell their goods. It's now possible to buy and even subscribe for a regular supply from a brand or of a product directly from the brand's site—which can be hosted on something like Squarespace, Shopify, and WordPress. Not only are you able to read about a coffee grinder or a razor on the *New York Times* website, you can buy it. You can buy the book you've read a review of on the *Wall Street Journal* site. Media outlets, among others, have begun to monetize their sites in this way, and they're not alone.

Airbnb rentals have capitalized on the traditional bed-and-breakfast model, making it easier than ever to list a room or house for rent, and making it easier than ever to find a place to stay when traveling. On top of that, many of those Airbnb rentals now offer toiletries for sale. If you forget your soap or shampoo, or happen to enjoy using a new brand you've never before tried, you can take it home with you.

Google, for one, holds one of the more powerful positions, in that they understand intent. Type in "brown sturdy hiking shoes," and Google not only delivers relevant advertisements but also lists ways to fulfill the transaction without even going to the retailer's site.

Through these new avenues, the shelf has grown exponentially. Retailers are no longer the exclusive owner of the shelf space, and by definition, therefore, of the consumer relationship. This provides brands with greater control over who sees and receives their product, as well as how they see and receive it.

Decentralization is only going to continue in the future. We're now heading into the notion of "invisible commerce," where products and services are purchased automatically without the consumer having to think about it. Amazon released the "Dash Button," a Wi-Fi connected device that reorders a consumer's favorite items by simply pressing a button. Recently, Amazon announced a deal to take things even further with Brother, GE, and Gmate. Now your printer will automatically order ink for you from Amazon when it is low and, most importantly, before you run out. Same goes for GE washing machines. New detergent will be ordered when you are running low. As will lancets and blood test strips for your Gmate glucose meter.

Now we're seeing commerce layers being added on top of services, such as UberRUSH, a delivery service run by Uber, or CPGs being able to sell its toiletries to Airbnb hosts and their guests. Although these services are not what Uber or Airbnb were originally designed for, we're seeing more and more layers of commerce added in, further distancing retailers from the conversation.

We are quickly heading to a world of unconscious commerce. Based on historical data and purchasing patterns, your transactions will happen by themselves. Utilizing massive data sets and your personal habits, merchants will be able to deliver goods to replenish your pantry without you even realizing they need replenishment.

This is not the end of the brick-and-mortar retailer. We still need retailers, although consumers' reliance on them is diminishing. If anything, retailers have an unbelievable opportunity, because they have vast fulfillment infrastructure already in place.

For something like a social media buy button to work, it needs three things: product listings and information, the ability to complete the transaction, and order fulfillment (the capacity and infrastructure to deliver the product to the customer). This is the basic skeleton of commerce. Where the information is coming from, who is completing the transaction, and how the order is being fulfilled are the most telling questions to determine who will succeed in the future. Retailers have decades of experience in retail and commerce, warehouses for fulfillment, and a significant amount of infrastructure to succeed in the now-decentralizing world. The first thing to think about is how to decentralize. There are plenty of options, ranging from turning huge brick-and-mortar locations into warehouses for fulfillment, to altering the physical locations to enhanced online sites that don't just sell a product but also provide an experience—namely, excellent customer service.

What's ahead in the coming decade is a land grab of sorts. Although not physical, brick-and-mortar locations, e-commerce sites and social media buy buttons are places we go and places people increasingly go to buy things.

Decentralization of commerce is like a leaky boat for retailers, and with new avenues multiplying so rapidly, it is impossible to plug all the holes. For brands, I believe this is the beginning of a golden age. When brands reach consumers directly, through social media or their own websites, the retailer is removed completely from the conversation, as are retailer's limitations and regulations. With the rise of decentralization, brands and retailers are now in a fight over where consumers end up, because in a connected world, people can wind up anywhere. Access to products, transactions, and information that the retailer does not own or control is the first piece of the puzzle that's started to dissipate thanks to technology.

Evolution of Commerce

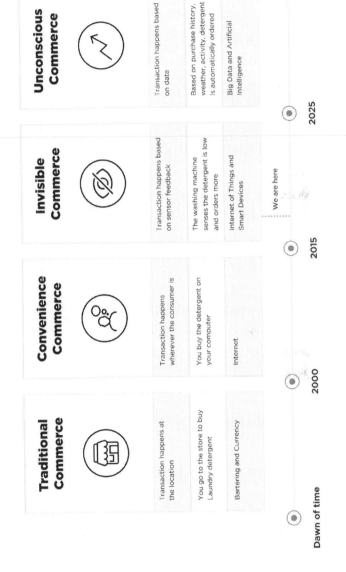

Traditional Commerce	Convenience Commerce	Invisible Commerce	Unconscious Commerce
Transaction happens at the location	Transaction happens wherever the consumer is	Transaction happens based on sensor feedback	Transaction happens based on data
You go to the store to buy Laundry detergent	You buy the detergent on your computer	The washing machine senses the detergent is low and orders more	Based on purchase history, weather, activity, detergent is automatically ordered
Bartering and Currency	Internet	Internet of Things and Smart Devices	Big Data and Artificial Intelligence

We are here

| Dawn of time | 2000 | 2015 | 2025 |

In addition to the notion of decentralization, the second factor leading to a changing environment is a leveling of the playing field, which leads to an enhanced ability to discover new things, and the rise of consumer awareness. Previously, products were discovered through advertisements in print media, television, or on the radio, plus a small fraction of word-of-mouth recommendations. The discovery of products was narrowed to brands whose marketing budgets were large enough to cover the most airtime. With the rise of technology, all of that has changed.

There is more information available than ever before, and the appetite for information has increased alongside its availability. Now we are more knowledgeable and understanding, with the ability to discover new products, all the while carried by an underlying discernment: we only want the best available product, or the best available price. Consumers can now easily figure out the specific ingredients in everything they eat, the fabrics they're wearing and where they were sourced, the exact location of where the gears on their bicycle were manufactured, and brands commitment to the environment or charitable efforts. We're seeing a convergence of content, access to content, and desire for that content.

With smartphones, we have access to information in our pockets. Not only can I look up the ingredients in a product, but I can, in many cases, find out where those ingredients were sourced. I can research a brand's backstory easily and quickly. I can find out immediately if there is a massive recall. If I'm thinking of buying something from a company but learn that they recently caused a chemical spill with far-reaching impacts, I might chose a more ethical alternative.

As consumers, we are empowered with more information than ever before. Plus, we possess constant connection to our friends and the perpetual stream of social media—both can inform us of new products and brands. As a brand, we are able to communicate directly with an audience, find out what people are saying, what they think they need, and then fulfill that need.

No longer are people relegated to discovering new products while visiting a retailer or seeing a television ad. And immediately after discovering something, I have direct access to it, whereas before there was a disconnect: if I heard about something at a dinner party, I would have to wait until the next day, at least, to go and see it at the store. Now it's instant; someone can tell me about a product over coffee, I can look it up on my phone right then and there, and purchase it with a single click. With the rise of social media, the whole world is an ongoing dinner party discussion, and I can connect to all of them: reading reviews online, tracking social media channels, and e-mailing links to friends and family. Everything is happening on a much larger scale.

Alongside the rise of awareness comes a massive shift regarding the notion of value. Before, there was a race to the bottom, with consumers shopping various channels in order to find the cheapest price. Now there's a larger focus on the concept of value. Instead of simply shopping by price, consumers read blog reviews, Amazon user reviews, and form an opinion of the product based on other people's experiences. Research clearly shows that a huge majority of consumers—70 percent, in fact—prefer to get their information from their own research or their own phone, versus talking to a salesperson or human in a store. That means we're more empowered than ever, and we're empowered at the moment we need it most: the moment we decide to make a purchase.

Decentralization of commerce has created more outlets for buying, and consumer awareness means those outlets are more visible. Both of these factors are contributing to meaningful changes in market share. We're now seeing power shifting away from big brands and into the hands of smaller players. When Dollar Shave Club launched in the summer of 2011, providing a direct-to-consumer subscription service for men's razors and shaving supplies, Gillette's iron grip on the North American men's grooming market withered almost 10 percent over just a couple of years. Although it may seem like they were an outlier, Dollar Shave Club is not alone. More and more craft brands are challenging the market share of massive companies, proving that we're in the midst of some revolutionary and tectonic shifts in commerce.

UNSTOPPABLE: THE FORCES BEHIND THE NEW WORLD

Retailers were like islands: physical destinations, and only so many from which to choose. But now, more and more islands are popping up with this notion of decentralized commerce. As a retailer, continuing to do what you've done well is important, and using existing tools to maximize reach and impact is great—but not if it means ignoring the rise of other islands all around you.

It's tempting to believe that with the right promotions or marketing plans, big businesses and retailers can hold onto their market share, maintaining the status quo. It's also tempting to think that craft brands are a fad, when in reality this new world is driven by some deep systematic changes in the economy.

THE CHANGING CONSUMER

People today are more conscious about what they're buying and not just from a price perspective. Directly related to the severity of the 2008 recession, people became more aware of where their hard-earned dollars went. A new generation of consumers came of age at that time, innately curious about what's in a product, what makes it worthwhile, and what makes that vendor special. Seven or eight years have passed since that brutal economic downturn. Things are better, and consumers who were sixteen- or seventeen-year-olds during the recession are now in their twenties and have become a demographic less focused on material things and more focused on quality goods and experiences. They're seeking fewer goods of better value, and in many cases, those goods have meaning for them.

People are happy to spend ten dollars on something they think is worth fifteen, but not when it comes to spending five dollars on something they think is worth one dollar. It's no longer strictly about cost but perceived value—and not just the value of ingredients or materials but also the story behind them. The leading brands of tomorrow will not only provide unique products of quality, but they will couple them with narratives, whether it's a commitment to the environment, community, or human rights. This is no longer a fringe movement of environmentalists or hipsters, but something we're seeing as a consequence of a cautious economic time.

Although we've seen a huge shift in the last few years toward e-commerce, with more sites launching every day and more options for brands to sell direct to consumers, this does not mean we'll be seeing the end of brick-and-mortar anytime soon. If anything, physical locations are more important than ever and represent a golden opportunity for retailers and brands to offer consumers an experience, more so than a simple purchase. At a retail location, you can see the product in person, hold the physical item, talk to someone about its specifications, ask questions, gain information, and check out or discover other things you might not have found if you were searching online. Losing this experience would be a huge detriment to both consumers and retailers. It is interesting to note than many leading e-commerce companies like eyeglass maker Warby Parker, menswear shop Bonobos, jewelry site Blue Nile, and even Amazon have opened bricks and mortar "extensions" to their online presence in order to provide customers with a richer, more immersive experience.

We're quick to forget that the physical experience compliments an online experience. Technologies such as mobile phones give consumers more power and access to information than ever before. There is no longer just a desire for deeper stories about the products that surround us; there is an expectation.

EVER-INCREASING DISTRIBUTION CHANNELS

Technology is not just a great equalizer for consumers. New technologies are enabling brands to optimize and work more efficiently with their existing retailers, while seamlessly entering other avenues and channels. It used to cost millions to bring a product to market: organizing a sales team to serenade buyers at retailers, setting up manufacturing facilities and warehouses for fulfillment, connecting with distributors, and advertising to consumers. Now small brands are enabled by technologies, whether it means using an outsourced manufacturer, listing on marketplaces such as eBay or Amazon, and advertising for pennies or dollars through social media networks.

Decentralization of commerce is great for small brands, allowing them to get products listed and to generate revenue streams quicker and cheaper. Instead of needing a ten-million-dollar Super Bowl advertisement, brands can increase visibility through social media by listing a video on YouTube for free, maintaining Twitter, Instagram, and Facebook accounts. That visibility allows for a greater brand awareness at a much lower price of entry than ever before, as well as the ability to create entire communities around products, such as GoPro, World of Angus, and Lululemon, to name a few.

Connected, smart devices will further drive this dynamic. Electronics and sensors collect data and allow for more streamlined, curated commerce. For example, if I'm running a 5K with a wearable device like a smartwatch, it can direct me to the closest place to buy a sports drink. This idea of an "Internet of Things" is yet another example of islands of decentralization cropping up, where commerce can happen outside of typical trips to the retailer. Instead of ordering a product from your laptop or mobile phone, simply press the Dash Button, and your account is charged, and the product is on its way to you. Taking this another step further are appliances that sense when a container is nearly empty and then automatically reorder it for you.

We've even reached a point where the data being collected about a consumer enables suppliers to identify what they need when they need it. For example, Amazon can determine—based on collected data regarding usage of products—how much Tide detergent I use in any given season and when I need to reorder. Based on my past buying behaviors, the product is ordered for me and shows up at my door. I call this "unconscious commerce."

Lastly, with 3-D printers now affordable for the home, we're able to print a select amount of goods immediately. Colette Patterns, for instance, is one of many garment and apparel pattern companies that allow you to print patterns as PDFs on demand. And if you have kids who love Lego blocks, you probably lose a bunch of pieces every few months. With your 3-D printer, the missing pieces could be recreated, automating the fulfillment aspect of commerce.

All of these are new points of contact for commerce that are outside the typical retail store or e-commerce site.

MORPHING BUSINESS MODELS

The way products are priced and sold is changing as well. The last few years has seen the rise of the subscription model. Although many of us grew up familiar with print magazine subscriptions, we're now seeing that same model being applied to a broad range of goods. Instead of buying snacks, shaving supplies, or beauty products each time you run out, companies will send them to you on a weekly or monthly basis for a flat fee, providing you with continuous access to your favorite products and the ability to discover new ones without having to leave the comfort of your home. Instead of buying DVDs, you subscribe to Netflix. Instead of going to Sephora to check out makeup, you subscribe to Birchbox. Instead of running out to the corner store for snacks when that midafternoon craving hits, you subscribe to Graze. Instead of heading to the grocery store or farmer's market for your favorite coffee, you subscribe to Craft Coffee.

Subscriptions are taking the place of what used to be large, upfront expenses. The sharing and subscription economy provides options for people who may have been hesitant to buy products because of their price-to-use ratio. If you're building a dining room table, it doesn't make sense to buy the whole set of tools—a drill, a table saw, a power cleaner—if you think you'll only use it once. Instead, you can rent them by the day or per project. Likewise, if you're going on vacation and want to take really great photographs, you can rent equipment rather than splurge on a fancy camera.

Most importantly, you no longer need to rent them from a retailer. There are subscription services that give you access to almost any type of equipment. Even more unique is that there are technology platforms that allow you to rent items from other consumers who own them and would like to make a few extra dollars while the items are not in use.

Should you decide to lease a new car, you might choose to offset part of your monthly payments by becoming a driver for UberX—an overlap of both the subscription economy and sharing economy. If you live in a major metropolitan area, you no longer need to own or lease your own car. Subscribing to a car sharing service such as Zipcar can, in many cases, make it easier and more economic to live without your vehicle. If you own a house or condominium and don't need all the space, but you don't want permanent roommates, you can rent out a room on Airbnb.

The majority of new subscription models are direct-to-consumer sales. Since the launch of Dollar Shave Club and the resulting shift in market share in men's grooming, Gillette has launched its own shave club. Generally, these new models are adopted by and work well for brands, as opposed to retailers.

None of this is truly groundbreaking in that the sharing economy has existed forever, but now it's occurring on a larger scale. Historically, farmers used to pool their money to buy or rent heavy equipment or machinery, and then share it during various seasons. Communities all over the world still practice this. Airbnb is another example of a new take on something traditional: for years, people hosted travelers at bed and breakfasts, but now it's happening more efficiently than ever before. We're seeing a convergence of the subscription model with technology, making it possible to discover places to stay, easily book and pay for services, and share physical items.

THE BLURRING OF BRAND AND RETAILER

Brands and retailers used to be two very distinctly different things. Brands sold their products to retailers, who then made sure it reached the consumer. Now, with brands able to sell directly to consumers and retailers competing with countless channels, the line between brand and retailer is blurred.

The Age of Spiritual Machines by Ray Kurzweil, published in 1999, is a prescient glance into the future. The author describes one individual at the beginning of every chapter. Throughout the novel, the human has different parts of his body replaced or enhanced. It might be a cochlear implant for hearing or a bionic limb for an amputee. Kurzweil's point in all of this was to ask a precise yet complex question. At what point does this person become a new human? Is this the same person, just enhanced, or is this an entirely new being?

Kurzweil's book relates to a long-standing philosophical debate regarding a ship, and how, if you replace one plank because it's broken and then continue to do so as more pieces break, at what point is it considered an entirely new ship and not just an enhanced version of the original one?

We're seeing this analogy with commerce. Brands used to sell to retailers, who sold to consumers. But if brands are selling directly to consumers, does that make them retailers?

On the World of Angus website, you can buy the brand's shampoos. Since the brand was launched in 2015, it has added complementary partners, such as Petcube, which is a connected hardware device that allows you to watch and interact with your pets while you're at work or out of your home, even play with them using laser pointers, and Canada Pooch, which offers stylish jackets and boots for dogs. World of Angus now curates companies such as these alongside their own products, making it a destination for dog owners. At what point does World of Angus become a retailer, as opposed to a brand with its own private label? Now, it seems, everyone is a retailer, and everyone is a brand, especially as retailers launch their own private labels.

Previously, the only merchants were the retailers that sold

to consumers, but with brands selling directly, we're now seeing "merchant" become an umbrella term to describe anyone who sells to consumers.

There also seems to be an identity crisis among brands and retailers. There is a debate about the importance of the experience versus the importance of the transaction. Specifically, the battle to determine who owns the experience on the path to purchase and who owns the transaction (and, ideally, who can do both).

As recently as December of 2015, Johnny Sole, an independently owned shoe boutique in Oregon received a staggering amount of customers coming in to try on boots and shoes, only to have them leave and complete the purchase online through a web-only merchant. Johnny Sole doesn't offer online sales, as handmade and bench-crafted shoes and boots each vary in size and leather. Given that there are plenty of outlets to shop—online with Amazon, in person at department stores such as Nordstrom, and even the brand's website—customers were well-equipped with the specific style and color of what they wanted, as well as the lowest price available. The store had a hard time keeping up with who was selling what and for how much. It's impossible to carry every style and price match every merchant. So what's a traditional retailer to do to compete, let alone survive?

A couple of years ago, people started going to places like BestBuy to get a feel for products, see the selection firsthand, and have the visual or audio experience but then leave and order on Amazon. One solution for some retailers was to block Wi-Fi access in stores, or to drop the price to compete. But most retailers can't compete on price when margins are so thin, especially if they have physical locations with overhead.

For traditional retailers, the key is figuring out what they're really good at and maximizing that. In the case of Johnny Sole, and many retailers, they have a wealth of experience selling directly to consumers—more than most brands. They also benefit greatly from having a physical location. That way, retailers can attract passersby looking on a whim and have the product in stock for consumers to evaluate and buy for immediate gratification. Quite possibly, the greatest opportunity for traditional retailers, the linchpin, is in providing an experience, where it's not just about the product itself, but the process of trying something on, learning about the product from a knowledgeable sales-person, and leaving with it in your hands and being able to garner satisfaction from its use right away. To stand out, and thrive, retailers need to figure out a way to make that experience unique and memorable—excellent customer service, relevant information, a positive atmosphere—so that customers won't want to go anywhere else.

In addition to understanding consumers and being able to offer up an in-store experience, retailers have a huge opportunity surrounding the delivery of a product, commonly referred to as fulfillment. Having operated for decades, they understand what it takes to get products onto the shelves and to get those products into the hands of customers. Many have spent years cultivating relationships with brands and their representatives, ensuring consistent access to products and assistance. Big retailers with distribution centers across North America have a huge opportunity to maximize this strength and further leverage their infrastructure.

Big box stores and one hundred thousand square-foot locations may not necessarily be the way of the future. Instead, those locations could focus on two areas of commerce: first, the experience and second, fulfillment. Retailers are in a unique position to accommodate orders from various channels of decentralized commerce.

Not all brands are transitioning away from physical locations and exclusively onto the Internet. Warby Parker identified immense consumer frustrated regarding the high cost of eyeglasses and started offering frames and lenses at a significantly lower cost than most in 2010. The company designed frames in-house and started off selling direct to consumers through their website, offering a free home try-on and return service, coupled with their charitable initiative of providing eyeglasses to nonprofits. Not sure how you would look in a pair of their frames? Simply upload a photo of yourself to their website and use the online tool to "try on" the glasses—that is, overlay the image of the frame on your face. Then order five pairs to try on at home for free. To their credit, Warby Parker continued to challenge their own thinking on the new world of decentralized commerce. They recognized that there was still something missing from the online experience they were serving up and that they were missing out on a sizable portion of their available market. By 2015, Warby Parker had opened retail locations in sixteen states. Online clothing companies Frank & Oak and Indochino have done the same. Most recently, in November of 2015, Amazon opened its first brick-and-mortar location, proving that even e-commerce giants understand the importance of physical storefronts.

MAKING A GREAT CRAFT BRAND

As the pressure of market forces pushes brands to be more unique and the flourishing of craft brands continues, it is only going to become more challenging for long-standing brands to stand out. The easiest way to do so is to be better than someone else, whether that's in terms of operations, materials, processes, or price. Maybe your product is far superior than what's on the market because you've implemented a new technology—like how Under Armour's Storm technology enables cotton hoodies to be waterproof. Maybe you stand out because of a commitment to the environment, or to charitable causes. Whatever it is, key points to craft brand success can be boiled down to two things: quality and resonance.

Craft brands are started for a reason. One reason is an unmet need in the marketplace, where there is little to no competition and an opportunity to create new categories or solve a consumer problem. Another is when existing companies are doing something similar, but a craft brand believes they can do it better, or differently. Regardless of the reason, there's usually a compelling story behind it. The ability to identify the difference and the story is a way to convey the value of a product or brand.

Consumers are increasingly interested in value. People want to buy fewer, often more expensive products if it means they have a higher quality, as opposed to needing to repurchase cheaper products of a lower quality. A brand can create perceived value by offering an incredibly well-made product that solves a problem, or by creating products with stories that resonate, often in emotional ways, with the consumer.

Quality is typically defined as the standard of something as measured against other similar things, or the degree of excellence, or distinctive attributes or characteristics possessed by something. Quality in commerce can be the standards or facets of the materials, such as waterproof cotton hoodies, hand-stitched and Goodyear-welted soles, or the hundred-year-old processes used by Horween Leather Company in Chicago, which supplies leather for Timberland, Chippewa, and Wolverine boots, as well as major sporting goods companies.

The idea of quality in commerce is not reserved for garments and accessories. For instance, Open Farm Pet Food not only controls the processing of the meat used in its products but also has full visibility into its supply chain so it can trace where the meat originated and even the feed that went into the animal. Their website explains that the "entire farm-to-bowl supply chain is audited and certified by third-party organizations specializing in humane animal care and sustainable farming practices." Meaning they're not only concerned with what your pet is eating, but how the animals are treated and how the farm is run. It is a more holistic and thoughtful approach to dog food and a story that resonates with many consumers of today.

Although some people equate quality with health, such as stripping out gluten, carbohydrates, sugar, or fat, there are other brands maintaining that quality food upholds the tradition and integrity of an ingredient. Operating since 1925 in Ontario, Sterling Creamery takes "butter seriously—naturally." Crafted using local sweet cream and artisanal processes, the butter is 84 percent fat. Chefs swear by it.

Quality can be broken down into three categories: superior materials, better-sourced ingredients, and sustainability.

Levi's is a good example of the latter, having recently made a shift in terms of how they manufacture jeans. It's easy to forget that it takes water to make everything: water to feed chickens to lay eggs, water to grow oranges for juice, water to grow tea and coffee. Shockingly, nearly 3,800 liters of water are used during the lifecycle of a single pair of jeans—from growing the cotton, dying, and manufacturing, to consumer care and maintenance. Levi's figured out a process to reduce the usage of water by up to 96 percent in certain products and partnered with Water. org in the process.

It takes...

10 liters of water to make one sheet of PAPER	**40** liters of water to make one slice of BREAD
70 liters of water to make one APPLE	**80** liters of water per dollar of INDUSTRIAL PRODUCT
91 liters of water to make one pound of PLASTIC	**120** liters of water to make one glass of WINE
140 liters of water to make one cup of COFFEE	**1,300** liters of water to make one kilogram of WHEAT
4,800 liters of water to make one kilogram of PORK	**10,855** liters of water to make one pair of JEANS
15,500 liters of water to make one kilogram of BEEF	**16,600** liters of water to make one kilogram of LEATHER

Source: IBM

The company's usage of water might not be a selling point for most consumers. For some, a buying decision might be made because of the way something fits or feels. Maybe a consumer cares that it uses a certain kind of cotton, or maybe the selling point is that a bunch of celebrities wear it, or it's popular in the skateboarding community, or the price point is right because it's mass-produced.

In comparison, Tellason manufactures raw selvedge denim in San Francisco, using cotton and other materials sourced from the East Coast of the United States. "Raw" means the "fabric has not been wet processed or manipulated in any way prior to purchase." Because of this, "the wearer determines the aging characteristics of their jeans." Tellason boasts that, "after just a few days of wear, the jeans become completely personal and unlike any other pair in the world." The raw nature of the denim also means that Tellason uses less water in its manufacturing. Although their products are pricier than those of Levi's, the company advises consumers to consider the cost-per-use, stating that raw denim will last longer than preprocessed materials.

By comparing Tellason and Levi's, we're able to see how brands within the same product category express quality. For Levi's, value is expressed as classic jeans made with a consideration for the environment and sold at an accessible price. For Tellason, value and quality are determined by the materials and processes used, as well as where their manufacturing is based.

Different things resonate with different people. For some, Tellason's commitment to US-based manufacturing and quality materials resonates. For some, Levi's commitment to the environment and charitable giving begets resonance. For some, TOMS shoes' charitable mission really resonates, with their buy-one-pair, donate-one-pair to a child in need philosophy. For some, it's the thrill of finding something at a good price. Within a knitting community, there will be inveterate, dyed-in-the-wool fans of locally made yarn, or people who swear by certain blends of wools, while others who are allergic to the material opt for silk, linen, or synthetics. If we look at three consumers who each purchased the same sweater, one might be excited about what a great deal it was, another might love the material, and the third might feel passionate about the processes with which it was made—using lamb wool harvested from sheep in the Nepalese Himalayas.

Retailers have understood this for decades, which is why they've acted as curators of products. Johnny Sole in downtown Portland has been curating shoes and boots for twenty-three years with the understanding that what resonates with one customer doesn't resonate with another.

One woman might fall in love with a pair of Jo Ghost boots, handcrafted in Italy and hard to find, while another might fall in love with the comfort of Kork-Ease. It is not the brand's job to cater to everyone; it is the retailer's job to ensure there is a varied amount of products represented in order to appease a wider audience.

It's different for everyone, but there is one commonality: each product, each brand is accompanied by a story that makes it unique. You want the consumer to say, "This is why I bought this." Whether it's the cost or the details, there is an emotional attachment. You cannot fully predict resonance, nor can you possibly resonate with every single consumer. Ultimately, to be successful, a craft brand needs to figure out how it defines quality and value, which in turn needs to translate into a story for the consumer.

Craft beer thrived because of its story, which often included a commitment to quality, a passion about the product, a consideration for the environment, a priority to buy local, and a sense that something was at stake for the brewers.

For one, there was an assumption that small-batch brews are of a better quality than mass-produced beer. Both the hands-on approach to brewing and the ability to invest in higher-quality or more unique ingredients allowed brewers to distinguish themselves from the mass manufacturing of large multinational brewers. By scaling down the manufacturing, brewers were able to provide closer care and attention to the finished product.

This was the case with the Portsmouth Brewery, founded in Portsmouth, New Hampshire, in 1991 by siblings Peter and Janet Egelston. To this day, the Portsmouth Brewery only serves beer on tap that is brewed in-house, with the occasional exception of brews from their sister brewery, Smuttynose. The restaurant and bar offers tours of the modest brew facility, sources menu ingredients from local farms, and supports local charitable organizations. When the company first opened, the brewery's spent grain and hops were picked up by a local farmer to be used as animal feed. The restaurant has since implemented composting.

Still pretty obscure, the Portsmouth Brewery gained notoriety in the beer world with the release of Kate the Great, a Russian Imperial Stout. A limited batch of nine hundred hand-filled bottles sold out in six hours in 2008, with the next release scheduled for the following year. In 2012, fifteen thousand tickets were sold in less than twenty-four hours for a chance at being able to buy one of two thousand hand-filled bottles, with all of the proceeds being donated to charity. One attendee who flew in from San Francisco told the *Boston Globe,* "It's a great beer, but it's more about the experience." This proves that today's consumers aren't interested in things as much as they are in experiences.

Kate the Great's creator, head brewer Tod Mott, resigned to create his own brewery in nearby Kittery, Maine, called Tributary. Tributary Brewery's website says, "Experience Is Everything." The Portsmouth Brewery, its sister company Smuttynose, and Tod Mott's new Tributary Brewery are all great examples of why and how craft brands can be successful. The Portsmouth Brewery is the perfect storm of quality ingredients, attentive manufacturing processes, community outreach and support, commitment to sustainability, and emphasis on local. Tributary is the archetypal story of one man leaving a secure, distinguished position as head brewer in order to strike out on his own to pursue a passion. Again, we're seeing the backstory as an integral part of the brand, and although the brewery's approach is focused and niche, it attracts a wide audience. The humble beginnings story may resonate with certain consumers, some find it important to pay attention to the environment, and others just like really well-made beer.

What differentiates a craft brand is the unique story it tells. A brand fails when it panders to large audiences and tries to appease the masses. Craft brands need to tightly hone their products, curate their stories, nurture their most passionate ambassadors, and then let everything bloom from there. TOMS shoes is one such example of a brand that started out very small and obscure by mobilizing a handful of people who were really passionate about the cause and the shoes. Eventually, with a brand that has this kind of integrity, a critical mass develops that allows it to break through to the next level and into the mainstream. If TOMS had initially tried to be everything for everyone from the get-go, they likely would not have reached such a velocity and been as successful.

We can learn a lot from successful craft brands such as TOMS, the Portsmouth Brewery, Tellason, Levi's, Sterling Creamery, and Open Farm. What makes a good story or a successful brand isn't just one thing. Usually it can be broken down into eight tactics that craft brands can utilize for success: selling direct to consumer, poking the bear, adding value, creating a community, building a fanatic-user base, differentiating through service, establishing lean manufacturing, and pursuing a mission. These are not abstract ideas, but eight tactics that have been employed successfully.

These tactics were determined by careful consideration of successful craft brands. The strategy or goal of creating a successful craft brand is not based on mass production, but instead focusing on a core audience where product quality and the story resonate.

PART II

—

SMALL
WONDERS

SELLING DIRECT
TO CONSUMER

Imagine this: It's 1901, you're a man, and you need to shave. The razor you own was passed down to you from your father, who got it from his father. It's one of the oldest things you own, and like most of what you own, every member of the family has used it. It's kept on a shelf beside a small mirror and a container of soap above a basin in a chilly room that acts as the bathroom. Sitting beside it is a strap of leather, which you strike the blade on each day to sharpen it. But the leather isn't cutting it anymore.

It's the dead of winter in your town not far from Boston, Massachusetts. You suit up in your warmest clothes to collect snow from outside. You melt it in the basin. The snow is the cleanest water you'll have all year. Once it melts, you take the razor from the shelf. You run your thumb over the blade and discover you couldn't even slice into an apple with it—it's duller than dull.

You know you need to shave. You know you need to leave the warmth of the wood stove, brave the cold, and bring the razor to be sharpened. You could wait for the traveling knife sharpener, but he won't be coming by until the roads clear in the spring.

A gentleman by the name of King Camp Gillette couldn't stand going into town to get his razor sharpened every few weeks. The late 1800s saw men frequenting barbers to have their bears and mustaches trimmed or using a straightedge razor at home, which needed to be taken in and sharpened. Seeing there was a hole in the marketplace, Gillette invented the first safety razor by "clamping a smaller version of a straight edge onto a handle." This made it not only replaceable when dulled, but easier to control. This double-edged disposable safety razor changed the face of shaving. Suddenly, at the turn of the century, a man no longer needed to leave the house to have a sharp blade. Instead, he could purchase a razor handle and a bunch of disposable blades.

Gillette clearly hit on something huge. It was so popular, men shelled out half their weekly pay for a razor and blades. The average pay in 1901 was $10 per week, and Gillette priced the razor at $5. In today's dollars, that would be around $150. It was so revolutionary, and such a crucial new piece of technology that provided convenience, that men paid a fine price for it.

Gillette sold a staggering seventy million units in 1915. Proctor & Gamble acquired the company for $57 billion in 2005. Gillette pioneered a concept that we see all over now: the most important purchase is the recurring one. For instance, a company can make profit off of a Brita water system, an espresso or a Keurig coffee machine, but the most important and consistent source of profit are the cartridges and filters. The filter, the coffee pod—that's the recurring business. King Camp Gillette's disposable razors pioneered that type of business model.

Shaving has come a long way since Gillette's invention in the early 1900s. What started as an eponymous craft brand has flourished into one of the leading companies for men's shaving that boasts a wide range of products and materials and is always on the cutting edge of new technologies.

Still, despite all the new technologies, it took another

110-plus years to revolutionize the shaving industry again the way Gillette did initially in 1901. Instead of going out to buy disposable cartridges or blades, a few clever entrepreneurs asked the simple question, "Why can't the blades now come to you?"

Imagine this: It's 2012. The experience of shaving has not significantly evolved in decades. Some might even say it's worse. Sure, there are more pharmacies and retailers providing access to razors and blades, but you still find yourself running out of them at the most inconvenient times. You bought a new handle with five disposable cartridges for what felt like a billion dollars. Those first four cartridges were changed frequently, and you reveled in the feeling of a clean shave—something you had forgotten was such a simple luxury. That last razor cartridge though, lasts you three months. You ignore the blade's dullness, the peeling of the lubricated strip along the top. You ignore it until you can't anymore: It's three in the morning, and you just finished preparing for a big meeting in the coming hours. While brushing your teeth, you notice in the mirror that you desperately need a shave—it's the one preparation you neglected.

You drag yourself from the comfort of your house to the pharmacy. The dark parking lot gives way to brightly illuminated aisles, so bright it's blinding. You locate the razor aisle in a string of aisles filled with stuff you're not sure you need or will ever need, but it's nice to know it's there. Finally, you find it: the razor and blade display case. It's the Fort Knox of display cases. Thick plexiglass encases packages of razors and cartridges. You wonder if the plexiglass is bulletproof. Probably flameproof. You press the small button beside the case that says "Ring for assistance." You wait. When no one arrives, you ring the button again. Are there even any other customers in the store? It's three in the morning. How can they be busy?

Finally, you lift the lid, knowing you can reach the bottom-most container of cartridges—never mind that they aren't the ones you usually use. Air raid sirens blare. Alarm bells make you jump. The lid shuts, and your chance at cartridges is ruined. You are asked to leave the store.

Or, if you do succeed—that is, if someone arrives to open the case—you are asked to point to the blades you want. You feel like you're in a lineup identifying a criminal, but feeling like one also. The store associate doesn't dare hand you your desired purchase because store policy requires them to carry your blades to the checkout counter. The associate scans the package, bags it, and tells you it will be forty dollars for eight razor cartridges.

What's that? In your sleep-deprived stupor, you forgot

your wallet, and you only have a twenty-dollar bill stuffed in your pocket? The cartridges go back to the case, and you pick up a smaller package, knowing that those four will only last you a little while, and you'll be right back here all over again.

When you get home, you spend twelve minutes trying to hack into the package. You wish you had a flamethrower.

Amazingly, it took over a hundred years to change this. In response to frustration with the high cost of razors and blades, having to ask associates to unlock cases at retailers, forgetting to buy extra blades, unnecessary bells and whistles, and celebrity-sponsored products, Dollar Shave Club was born in 2012. The company's founder, Michael Dubin, posted a video on YouTube in March of that year. Within an hour, the company was so inundated with traffic, the site's server crashed. Within forty-eight hours, there were twelve thousand orders.

The video showed that Dollar Shave Club was something different—definitely not Gillette. Instead of a celebrity or a faceless, massive, monolithic entity, viewers saw an everyman—a guy whose speech was straightforward, whose look was not airbrushed, who joked, and who didn't break eye contact while he told them "Our blades are f***ing great." Not only that, the guy in the video was the founder himself, Michael Dubin, speaking directly to the viewer—which is exactly the point.

More videos were released with spoofs on the sometimes-traumatic experience of buying a razor and blades—complete with background checks, fingerprinting, and tasing. The humor in those videos lies in their similarity to the actual experience, which is uncomfortable—making one feel like a criminal. The videos also pointed out that consumers were paying a lot of money to feel like a criminal and for an experience that is definitely not rewarding.

Men care more about their grooming than ever before: in the United States and Europe, 86 percent of men say they prefer simple grooming routines. Responding to that need, Dollar Shave Club sells direct to the consumer, cutting out distributors and retailers and fancy advertising contracts in favor of good products sent directly to the consumer's home. No more going to the drugstore and having to ask an associate to unlock a display case once he or she eventually locates the supervisor with the key. No more forgetting to buy cartridges. No more useless add-ons. No more being inundated with choices. No more trying to decide which type is right for you. Dollar Shave Club takes the guesswork and the legwork out of buying razors and cartridges.

Dollar Shave Club has since landed multimillion-dollar investments, but its beginnings were modest. An article in the *New York Times* notes that cofounder Mark Levine had 250,000 twin razors he asked Dubin to help him sell online. Levine "had experience with product development and wholesaling," while Dubin helped "companies make promotional online videos." Both had relevant experience to help them build out the company, which essentially responded to a problem:

> *If you ask most guys how they buy razors, they talk about being frustrated with the price and the experience of going to the store to buy them. I saw a market need to solve that problem by making it easy for guys to get it done. It was never about recurring revenue. Guys are so used to milking their blades for as long as possible because they're so expensive, and they'd forgotten how awesome it can be to shave with a fresh razor each week.*

When it cuts out the retailer and sells directly, a brand can invest more in essentials: quality of materials and the product itself, as well as storytelling, packaging, and community building.

Dollar Shave Club was able to offer "f***ing great" razors at a reasonable price—razors unaccompanied by unnecessary add-ons that increase the cost of manufacturing.

Within a few years, they expanded to provide its own line of shave butter, hair products, and wet wipes—all with the intention of owning a man's bathroom shelf.

All of this was accomplished without a single account at a traditional retailer. Dollar Shave Club operates on a subscription model, where members pay a fixed amount for blades, which are automatically delivered to them at home or their place of work each month, or every other month. There are no subscription fees and no commitments, and shaving and hair products are exclusively available to members.

By offering products directly to the consumer, brands create a unique experience devoid of dependence on the retailer. As Dubin noted, men often feel "frustrated" with the experience of buying razors, even criminal—trying to help yourself to razors often leads to alarm bells ringing. With Dollar Shave Club, razors reach consumers in the comfort of their own homes. However, customers aren't just buying a thing, they are now members of a club. This direct-to-consumer model allows brands to create a community, and the consumer can take part in it without even having to leave the house.

Having your brand carried by a retailer often means having to conform to shelf-space restrictions and competing with other brands' packaging and pricing. You don't have to worry about it being brightly colored, or spending lots on design and marketing, or trying to keep it to a certain size. By selling direct to the consumer, you don't have to worry about theft restrictions—such as PVC plastic that takes a flamethrower to open. Not only is it frustrating to buy razors at the store, it's also nothing short of a physical challenge, as opening the package once one gets it home is often dangerous to one's fingers.

(Special author's note: If you haven't seen it, I strongly recommend watching the *Curb Your Enthusiasm* short video segment entitled, "Larry David vs Bad Packaging," which you can easily find on YouTube.)

Dollar Shave Club sends a customer a box, thereby owning that experience and that relationship with the consumer, as well as fully owning what comes in the box. Dollar Shave Club can write quirky, irreverent things on the packaging that would not fly at traditional retailers, but makes the experience much more personal for the consumer—as if part of an inside joke.

As a direct-to-consumer brand, you are not beholden to third parties changing your story, misrepresenting your product, or neglecting it. Instead, you are empowered to maintain the integrity of your unique brand and its relationship with your audience.

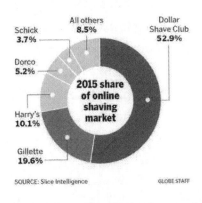

Schick
3.7%

All others
8.5%

Dollar
Shave Club
52.9%

Dorco
5.2%

**2015 share
of online
shaving
market**

Harry's
10.1%

Gillette
19.6%

SOURCE: Slice Intelligence   GLOBE STAFF

The global men's grooming market is estimated at $21.4 billion in 2016, and is speculated to grow to $26.6 billion by 2020. For a long time, Gillette has held most of the market share. In *Fortune* magazine, Gillette boasted that it had earned back 4 percent of online market share through its new shave club, which launched in the summer of 2015. That Gillette had to point out that it lost and then regained 4 percent of its market share highlights the importance of this new subscription-based business model. The *Financial Times* reported that Gillette has 21 percent of the online shaving market. Dollar Shave Club has 54 percent. That's a huge number. Dollar Shave Club was only launched in 2012 and grew to own 54 percent of online market share for men's shaving in only three years—taking share away from Gillette. Gillette now holds 60 percent share of the total men's grooming market, down from 70 percent not too long ago. A 10 percent drop is significant (equating to over two billion dollars in sales in 2016) and shows the kind of threat craft brands can be to the multinationals.

Dollar Shave Club has raised $163.5 million in funding

since its inception, with most of it coming from top-tier Silicon Valley venture capital (VC) firms. Investors consider the brand not to be a consumer product company, but a tech company. This is mainly due to its distribution model. Instead of storefronts, it has a dedicated website, and the focus is on maintaining and promoting it. VCs are investing in the company's growth as they see the swift rise of the brand.

A subscription business model is fascinating in that it has very basic economic metrics based on how much it takes to acquire a customer. You add the expenses of advertising, promotions, marketing, and sales teams to determine how much it costs to acquire one customer. Dollar Shave Club's blade subscription costs $12 per year for three years, with zero commitment. You can surmise in general terms that the lifetime value of a customer here is roughly $36, but there's also the opportunity to upsell. Given that their products are only available to members, they ensure that subscribers will not only meet their minimum customer acquisition cost, but hopefully exceed it with add-ons and premium services. Then you calculate the return: How many people will leave, or "churn" as it's commonly known in the industry, over time?

For every dollar you put in, you make $3 and lose $1. You put $1 in and walk away with $2. It doesn't matter if it's razor blades, software, or furniture; the only thing that matters is the formula—that's what people are investing in. It just so happens that Dollar Shave Club is in a large market that resonates with people.

When they started, Dollar Shave Club proved that their customer acquisition cost could be kept really low. Generally, a brand needs massive marketing budgets in order to run ads during popular television shows. Generally, to bring customers in, you need to spend a lot. For Dollar Shave Club, their video cost $4,500 and was broadcast on YouTube for free. That $4,500 brought in twelve thousand orders within the first forty-eight hours—under $0.40 per acquired customer. Having their video online meant that it could be watched more than once and easily shared. The video went viral, and the company never had to rely on acquiring customers through expensive, traditional media. At the time of this writing, the video had more than twenty-two million views on YouTube.

Dollar Shave Club has a simple value proposition. The subscription service is a dollar, which is a low barrier to get someone to put their credit card down. Then the company makes it easy to get other things—upsells, add-ons, and premium services. Once you have consumers hooked as consistent customers through a subscription service, you can increase their lifetime value and sell more to them on an annual basis. Even if they don't love it, the $1 per month is such a small risk that there is a very low risk of people leaving, and an even lower risk of the customer being disappointed.

Since Dollar Shave Club's inception in 2012, it has become a leader in the online men's shaving industry. With over two million subscribers, the company claimed in 2015 to have surpassed Schick in becoming the number two razor cartridge brand by volume. That same year, Gillette had no other choice but to respond to this new competitive threat and launched its own shave club that summer. It also flexed its financial muscle and slapped Dollar Shave Club with a lawsuit that December, alleging that Dollar Shave Club had stolen Gillette's patented technology. After only a few years in the market, there was no doubt that Dollar Shave Club had succeeded in poking the bear.

POKING THE BEAR

—

Josh Tetrick started food company Hampton Creek with the belief that "eating well should be easy." A Fulbright Scholar with a law degree, Tetrick spent seven years in sub-Saharan Africa working with nonprofits. He accepted a job with TOMS shoes upon his return to the United States. Shortly thereafter, he launched 33needs, a crowd-funding site for socially conscious start-ups. In 2011, he came up with the idea for Hampton Creek and took two years to develop and launch its first product: Just Mayo.

Entirely based on plant-based ingredients, formulated with non-GMO canola oil and wholly devoid of eggs, Just Mayo is a substitute for the egg-allergic, health-conscious, and vegan-friendly consumer (although Tetrick is a vegan, the term is conspicuously absent from the company's marketing). It debuted at Whole Foods Markets in northern California and has since reached the shelves of retailers such as Target, Costco, Safeway, and Walmart. In November of 2015, *Fortune* reported that Compass Group, a multinational contract food services company, would source baking mixes and dressings exclusively from Hampton Creek.

As the company's website extolls, Just Mayo is "so much more than a condiment." The name itself isn't meant to be read as *only* mayo, but "guided by reason, justice, and fairness."

Producing one egg requires over sixty gallons of water. Bill Gates invested in Hampton Creek on the basis that, "Our planet can't sustain the current rate of growth in animal-based foods." Food writer and chef Andrew Zimmern reviewed Hampton Creek's products on his site, noting that the United Nations reported that the global demand for eggs was fourteen million tons in 2000 and is projected to be thirty-eight million tons in 2030.

Hampton Creek not only considers the well-being of the environment but also the health of consumers. Just Mayo is cholesterol free, non-GMO, soy-free, gluten-free, and dairy-free, with no artificial coloring. Not to mention, no eggs means no risk of salmonella, plus ease in portability, and a longer shelf life.

What's not to like? Apparently, the name.

Similar to Gillette flexing its financial muscle on Dollar Shave Club, it only took one year after Just Mayo's release for Hellmann's to slap the company with a lawsuit. Hellmann's, owned by Unilever, held more than a third of the billion-dollar-plus mayonnaise market. The company alleged Hampton Creek was using false advertising and "unfair competition"—that they couldn't call their product "mayo" if it did not contain eggs. According to the civil suit, there were "'unsubstantiated superiority claims' [that] have 'caused consumer deception and serious, irreparable harm to Unilever.'"

Hampton Creek was not only offering an arguably higher quality and healthier product, but it was also offering it at a lower price. Clearly, Unilever and Hellmann's felt more than a little threatened.

Although the suit was dropped at the end of 2014, the "Mayo Wars," as it came to be called, did not end there. The Food and Drug Administration (FDA) sent Hampton Creek a warning letter in the summer of 2015 detailing offenses made by the company's "misbranding."

According to the FDA, "egg is a required ingredient" of mayonnaise, and Just Mayo "purport[s] to be a food for which a definition and standard of identity has been prescribed by regulation, but they fail to conform to such definition and standard."

By failing to conform, by finding ecologically sound alternatives to "standard" practices, Hampton Creek threatened the market share of a multinational corporation. Instead of damaging Hampton Creek, the media coverage of Unilever's lawsuit actually elevated the brand's products, legitimizing their work and lending them credibility. Suddenly, everyone was talking about Hampton Creek. Big media companies were covering the craft brand, and the start-up could hold the microphone during the conversation. People who had never even heard of Hampton Creek were hearing about their innovative product and healthier recipes. And the FDA, in asking Just Mayo to refine its branding, offered a unique opportunity for the brand to reiterate its message of health, well-being, and justice to consumers.

Hampton Creek is not ultimately out to hurt Unilever and Hellmann's or to simply make a buck. They're out to change the dynamics of the egg industry—a much bigger industry to disrupt. Just Mayo was just the beginning. Hampton Creek isn't an alternative condiment company;

it is an alternative egg company. Its plant-based egg substitute is disruptive to the egg industry, not simply the mayonnaise industry. To respond to the potential threat, the American Egg Board allegedly "launched a campaign against Hampton Creek that was beyond its mandate," which included trying to pull the product from Whole Foods shelves. The USDA began investigating the Egg Board in late 2015, while Tetrick and Hampton Creek prepared for the launch of the company's next product, Just Scramble, a plant-based egg substitute.

Poking the bear is not always the best or the right approach for a given brand. Some take a more overt approach, while others are more subtle. Hampton Creek's messaging was not overt like Dollar Shave Club's. Instead, the company constantly reinforced its commitment to quality. It was a big deal when Unilever sued, but an even bigger deal when they backed down and dropped the suit. For a multinational, that's a no-win situation: they look like bullies if they maintain the lawsuit, and they lose if they drop it.

Meanwhile, media outlets were reporting outbreaks of avian flu. Not only do people become nervous about ingesting poultry products, but there are shortages that call for substitutes like Just Mayo. Although consumers might not be thinking about the far-reaching effects of the poultry industry when picking up a jar of mayonnaise at the store, it's clear that Hampton Creek is by offering solutions to local and global problems, as well as providing another layer of value.

There are a lot of sleeping giants in the commerce world—big, established brands that have been around for a while that don't take notice when someone new moves to the block because they are too secure in their current positions. It is hard for small brands to compete with the huge advertising and marketing budgets of such companies. However, with the rise of new technologies that allow companies to quickly come to market and reach consumers for very low costs, poking the bear has turned into a viable strategy.

In the old world, brands had tight relationships with retailers, and if you angered one brand, it could mean a corporate shutout. As a young upstart, it wasn't a good idea to go after a company such as Proctor & Gamble, as it could "influence" retailers and possibly threaten to pull product if contracts weren't cancelled. Back then, that was a big deal.

But now, with the rise of direct-to-consumer sales and more channels to reach customers, that old model isn't relevant. Brands no longer have that kind of leverage with retailers, nor the ability to muscle competing brands. If

Gillette were to tell Walmart not to carry Dollar Shave Club products, the craft brand wouldn't really care, considering that it sells directly to over two million subscribers.

In its launch video, cofounder Michael Dubin asks, "Do you like spending twenty dollars a month on brand name razors? Nineteen go to Roger Federer." It was clearly a shot at Gillette, which has sponsored the tennis legend since 2007. Still staring straight into the camera lens, Dubin continues, "Do you think your razor needs a vibrating handle, a flashlight, a back scratcher, and ten blades?" The short answer is no. The long answer is that this is an overt example of poking the bear, as opposed to Hampton Creek's more subtle approach.

Big brands are more cautious than they once were, knowing smaller companies and craft brands now have the opportunity to have their voices broadly heard. Poking the bear allows craft brands to build attention while visibly taking on a major player, generating awareness and publicity, and enabling a new conversation. Sometimes, poking the bear doesn't even have to be overt. It can be as subtle as saying you're the healthier alternative.

Or, it could be as simple as totally avoiding the competition. Such is the case for Soylent, a perfectly balanced nutritional substance (in liquid or powder form) that can be eaten for breakfast, lunch, and dinner. Instead of offering a product similar or better than the competition, Soylent is saying, "You don't even need food." Just drink "full-balanced" shakes and supplements, which their website claims can be made in three minutes for three dollars a meal.

This takes poking the bear to another level. It's a blanket refusal to participate in the food system. Founded in 2013 and operating as a subscription service, the company received a boost when the FDA said that it had to be sold as food. In much the same way that Hampton Creek adds value by offering safe alternatives to poultry products, Soylent makes eating nutritional meals—if you can call them that—super easy and affordable.

ADDING VALUE

———

Frustrated by a lack of choices regarding pet products, Jeremy Potvin concocted World of Angus—named after his Boston Terrier–Jack Russel mix. Devoted to developing products from a dog's perspective, the brand was launched in 2015, first as a website dedicated to selling its own brand of dog shampoo directly to consumers. The site features bright product photographs, allowing viewers to read the succinct labels, which state that the product is biodegradable, chemical-free, and "gently scented using only essential oils."

The subtle messaging being conveyed here is that what we put on our skin—or the skin of our pets—is absorbed into our bodies and their bodies, as well as the ecosystems around us. Sulfates and chemicals can irritate skin and lead to a host of potential issues down the line—not to mention having harmful effects on the environment. There are over three thousand listings for "dog shampoo" on Amazon. But how many take into consideration issues of sustainability and health?

Jeremy Potvin's World of Angus shampoos set the bar higher for pet care. Using no sulfates, no synthetic chemicals or fragrances, the products take into account the health and well-being of pets, their owners, and the environment. Given that the ingredients are natural and biodegradable, the products are perfectly safe to use while camping by a river or lake. The cedar pine-scented shampoo acts as a natural bug repellent. The balm used to treat chapped paws is entirely edible. Their website adds, "You can feel good knowing you're not harming the environment your best bud loves to run around in." Potvin is quick to point out that the entire line is tested on humans first, even using the company's own staff to run product tests on themselves for a full week.

Also founded with the intention to reignite Canadian manufacturing, World of Angus manufactures locally in Toronto after going through five iterations of the product with several factories before settling on a factory the company liked. While developing its own products, the company reached out to other brands whose complementary products it wanted to pair with. By collaborating with brands that were already offering complementary services—such as Canada Pooch's dog coats and Filson's collars—World of Angus became more than just a place to find dog shampoo.

The brand expanded by selling its shampoos to retailers. The company understood the need to reach the consumer in the best way possible and in as many ways as possible.

Jeremy Potvin had the experience to start World of Angus quickly and efficiently. Having launched his own tech start-up, he had learned to listen to customers first and foremost. After running his own retail stores, he knew how to create a unique experience for the consumer. Although he wasn't opening a brick-and-mortar location, Potvin understood that giving his website visitors a great experience was a key component to the success of the brand. He was well aware the he would need to draw them there with more than just dog shampoo. Having previously founded technology company Shifthub in response to a problem (as a way to help employers manage hourly employee schedules), he created World of Angus in order to solve another problem: providing easy access to quality pet products, coupled with information and a community feel.

World of Angus focus on more than providing products to consumers through a website or retailer. First and foremost, the company focused on building the customer's trust. How? It built the world's largest and most extensive database of dog parks—3,872 in North America alone—and built apps so people can find places to take their dogs and socialize. They established two websites—AngusPost and LOLWoof—to provide a place to share content, curate links to stores and articles, participate in a conversation, and offer ideas and information about dogs. They actively maintain social media accounts as well, sharing photographs and stories as well as providing inspiration and connection for dog owners. The aim is to get these online platforms to become a jumping-off point for microevents, allowing people to connect with others in the community.

World of Angus is a great example of a brand that provides value on numerous levels. For one, it offers high-quality dog shampoo to discerning pet owners—people who are willing to pay more for quality ingredients that are safe for their pets, themselves, and the environment. The brand is also acting as a curator, bringing in complementary, well-made products to provide a well-rounded shopping experience—dog beds, dog coats, merino wool sweaters, and even boots for dogs—and paying attention to Canadian manufacturing. One customer might admire the company's commitment to manufacturing in North

America, another might feel passionately about the biodegradable ingredients, and someone else might see value in the pet care information gleaned from the company's blog or website.

Usually, when someone says the word "value," we equate it to cost. Now we're seeing a shift, where people consider not only the monetary value but also the benefits and significance. Like resonance, it's hard to predict what someone will dub valuable. For some, it may be the cost, but for others it is sustainability initiatives, or health-conscious ingredients, or a sense of community.

Successful craft brands find ways of adding value beyond their products. The idea is to pull people to your site for something more than just what you produce. For World of Angus, that means offering accessories, toys, and apparel from trusted brands, relevant news and information, and a community of pet owners. It may seem like the company is just in the business of selling dog shampoo, but World of Angus is about so much more than that.

Jeremy Potvin says the brand "gives twice before we ask for anything." That means giving people access to an extensive dog park database, providing information on grooming a dog at home, and connecting people within the same community. It's not actually about selling a product at all, but when the time comes to launch a new scent of shampoo, or a balm, the conversation has changed from, "Buy this thing," to "We made this cool product, and we hope you'll trust that we have your best interest in mind and try it."

Jeremy's core message is less and less about selling things and more and more about helping the community. He feels that there's a direct correlation between the more you help and the more you get back in terms of loyalty. The more you give, the deeper the relationship you have with your consumers, and the more they trust you in regard to a transaction. The nice thing about World of Angus and similar craft brands is that they're able to reach consumers on various levels while still staying focused on who they are and what they want to provide. World of Angus is not pandering to a wide audience, but they are available and accessible to consumers by posting content, responding to inquiries, and curating quality products.

The direct-to-consumer strategy offers new ways for brands to add value. Previously, it was the brand's job to link up with retailers and get the product into the hands of the consumer, with the main value proponent being the product itself. Now, with direct-to-consumer sales, successful craft brands are not just building a brand, but promoting a lifestyle.

Although no longer a craft brand, Timberland got its start as a family-owned business. Recently, it launched its Modern Trail campaign, encouraging people to share their versions of a "modern trail" on social media. The result is user-generated content and galleries of photographs, plus content on their blog with book recommendations and how-tos on layering and weatherproofing canvas coats. The company conceives and produces exclusive concerts and events to bring people together. What they are providing are services that endorse the lifestyle, rather than simply selling a product—recognizing that the decentralized commerce world revolves less around selling stuff and more about providing value to the community.

Instead of being solely motivated by sales, brands such as World of Angus are focused on partnering with consumers in solving a problem. They're saying, "Let me provide you with the right information and the proper services you need so that you view me as a partner versus someone trying to sell you something." This authenticity leads to long-term loyalty, bigger basket sizes, and more customers. In recognizing that consumers are hungry for information and then providing it, brands are doing themselves and their audiences both a favor.

CREATING A COMMUNITY

———

GoPro, the handheld high-definition action camera company, is now a household name with 2015 sales north of $1.6 billion. But only a few years ago, they were a craft brand going up against massive electronics manufacturers: people who were at the helm of photography and videography for decades, with huge research and development budgets, vast distribution channels, and a robust sales staffs. GoPro jumped into a well-established field.

Nick Woodman developed the first prototypes in 2001, which were crude 35 mm cameras with wrist straps that he wore while surfing for five months in Australia and

Indonesia. Two years later, having developed and patented the first models, Woodman manufactured little 35 mm cameras in China for $3.05 and began selling them for $30 each to surf retailers. He expanded by selling to specialty sports boutiques and appearing on QVC, the home shopping network. In 2006, GoPro made the transition to video, with the first version recording ten seconds of film without any audio.

To put it in context: this was three years before the first iPhone with video capability hit the market. Although Woodman's first innovations seem crude to us now, it is clear that the brand was way ahead of its time, offering a service and solution when no one else was.

The initial fanatic-user base, primarily composed of adventure athletes, started finding new, creative ways to use GoPro products, which helped the company expand to a larger audience. The documentary "Sunshine Superman" follows Carl Boenish, one of the first pioneers of BASE jumping. Boenish was passionate about filming everything: he loved the sport and wanted to share it with people. It was an otherwise lonely pursuit, but the more people watched his solo jumps, the more they connected with his experience, and the more interest the sport gained. GoPro was less about the products and more about the experiences and connections that could be created with its products.

Around the same time that GoPro appeared, YouTube was picking up steam as a leading video content site. The concept of being able to share your experiences with others, to pull together a group of people with similar lifestyles and interests, and to enable them to share their perspectives was still fresh. GoPro offered surfers, snowboarders, extreme and adventure sports enthusiasts a way to capture their experiences and share them with other people. It allowed individuals—often participating in singular, solo activities—a way to publish their experiences, connect with other people who were passionate about the same things, and learn more about the experiences of others. In a way, GoPro was promoting empathy.

The core community of initial advocates began to grow. As more and more people recorded their adventures, and more people were able to watch, GoPro started breaking into the mainstream—riding on the shoulders of a very passionate, very strong, and very solid user base.

It wasn't about the product itself—GoPro cameras were simple, easy to use, without a lot of bells and whistles. It was about the content: what people were able to capture. GoPro quickly caught on and started featuring and promoting content created by its tools. That changed the narrative, changed the story from, "Buy this thing" to, "Go live your life, share it, and connect with other people."

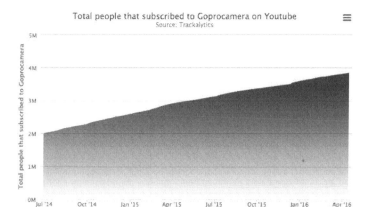

Total people that subscribed to Goprocamera on Youtube
Source: Trackalytics

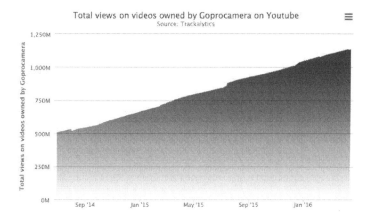

Total views on videos owned by Goprocamera on Youtube
Source: Trackalytics

A December 2015 video of Danny MacAskill navigating the rooftops of Gran Canaria on a bicycle is the perfect example of this.

The GoPro video was a collaboration between Mount Creative and Vision Ramps. It allowed the filmmakers to connect with the community of Gran Canaria in a really unique and memorable way (thereby allowing viewers a glance into a place they may have never heard of and providing a video that's probably better than any PR-firm's tourism advertisements), and it even spotlighted the music of California-based band the Dodos. Within a few months, the video had twelve million hits.

That community and the rhetoric around which GoPro was built became self-sustaining. The more people shared and connected, the more people wanted to share and connect.

Historically, a brand's relationship with the consumer was through a distributor and retailer, and the two almost never came face-to-face. Now, with the rise of direct-to-consumer sales, we're seeing brands and their consumers more intimately intertwined than ever. In that case, the relationship is one-to-one, but the beauty of community is that it includes many people connecting over a single goal or product.

Creating a community allows for better marketing and advocacy of products in ways that are impactful and cheap. Finding people who are like-minded to advocate for your product is key at the beginning, and if you get enough people, you'll reach a kind of critical mass—breaking through the ceiling and into the mainstream. But if you don't have a strong foundation—that core community—it is hard to launch into that next level.

Now, GoPro has reached the mainstream. Real estate companies attach the cameras to drones to get footage of new properties. This used to require the hiring of helicopters for decent aerial footage, and now we're able to get good footage with a simple little camera. People mount cameras on motorcycles and bicycles for footage of long rides, and daily commuters mount GoPro cameras on their helmets to capture footage of reckless drivers and accidents. Some strap them on their pets to see what the world looks like from their point of view. One person stuck a GoPro in a dishwasher to solve the mystery of what goes on when the door is closed and locked. Others have used GoPro cameras to capture footage of newsworthy events—giving way to a new community of citizen journalists.

GoPro has revolutionized all these other industries and areas that it was not initially set up for. Communities are taking these simple tools and coming up with their own concepts and ways to use them—ways that include new industries or disrupting old industries.

On October 12, 2014, an Austrian skydiver ascended into the stratosphere in a capsule attached to a balloon, jumped out, and free fell over twenty-four miles to Earth. Strapped to his pressure suit were seven GoPro cameras. The Stratos mission, which was covered by media around the globe due to it compelling and jaw-dropping video footage, was funded and sponsored by Red Bull.

While GoPro's beginnings were inside-out, letting the community develop the brand, Red Bull is the opposite—a sort of outside-in, where the brand and story are created, thereby drawing like-minded people to become part of the community. Red Bull, like GoPro, encourages people to push the envelope. Most know their catchy slogan, "Red Bull gives you wings." The Stratos mission was probably the most extreme and literal example of that: sending a man into space to free fall to Earth. Skydiver Felix Baumgartner broke three world records: the first human to break the sound barrier without any form of engine power, highest manned balloon flight, and highest altitude jump.

Nowadays, people think less of Red Bull as a drink or product and more of it as a set of experiences. For example, the yearly Flugtag ("flying day" in German) event challenges participants to "build and pilot home-made flying machines off a twenty-eight-foot high flight deck" built over a body of water. Red Bull also sponsors and hosts the Air Race World Championships, European Freeski Open, Burton US Open, concerts and music festivals, and Crashed Ice in which skaters race through an icy obstacle course.

Clearly, Red Bull is not about a drink. It's about kicking things up a notch. The Red Bull Stratos event was the most beautifully choreographed marketing event in the history of the world. The branding and live coverage were right in line with the Red Bull brand, as were the high stakes of the event. (It was not clear Baumgartner would survive the high-risk jump. There was a realistic chance that he might burst into flames upon reentering the earth's atmosphere). Ultimately, it had nothing to do with the energy drink and everything to do with providing value through shared and curated experiences.

BUILDING A FANATIC USER BASE

Although there are plenty of brands selling sports equipment, there are few focused solely on training. The California-based brand SKLZ "prepares athletes to be ready for their sport." Selling directly to consumers on the website, and making products available at major sporting goods stores and specialty retailers, SKLZ both provides the equipment and the inspiration to "train smarter." Rather than focus on hockey sticks, baseball bats, cleats, and products that other athletic companies produce—and produce well—SKLZ focused on nets for batting practice, poles for agility training, and medicine balls for resistance. Basically, anything you would find at practice, or at your local gym, but never thought about buying for yourself.

It's a very niche market and one that the people at SKLZ are well suited to cater to. The company's president, Brian Enge, spent fifteen years in the sports apparel industry, was senior vice president at Saucony, is active in the triathlon community, and coaches soccer. Enge is not alone. The entire staff has a background in sports and they still maintain active lifestyles: clocking up to two hundred miles on a bike per week, playing ice hockey, skiing, and running. The staff also includes a former pro-baseball player who now coaches with his two boys. Eighty percent of their employees were at least semipro athletes. Six were pro-athletes, and the company invites others to be involved in the development process. Clearly, a consumer can trust someone who is not only developing a product but also using it within the context of coaching and training.

It helps that almost all of the founders and staff of SKLZ were pro-athletes and continue to be athletic. It's deeply embedded in their culture to not just play sports but also to practice and train. They are an ace in an industry of people who are very passionate about what they do, and they are people who have sacrificed. They are the core audience for their brand, and their dedication is contagious.

A lot of craft brands spring up from the very fertile soil of passionate, fanatic-user bases. Like with GoPro, it starts with these advocates connecting with each other and bonding over the product and what it allows them to do. A fanatic-user base and a community are two different things. A community is a group of people who care about the same thing and have a common interest. Within it can be found a fanatic-user base, usually consisting of individuals who are super passionate advocates for the brand and its products.

Fanatic users are especially valuable to a craft brand because they are deeply committed to the product. They will pay a premium for quality and consistency, and they will be vocal supporters of the brand and its work. In the case of SKLZ, it's hard to imagine a coach or an athlete wanting to buy a nameless brand on Amazon when all of the equipment they need is available on one site, which offers consistency, convenience, and information in the form of training videos and relevant links.

Under Armour started as a craft brand in 1996, and in the last twenty years, it has grown to compete with big names such as Nike. Like SKLZ, athletes started Under Armour for athletes. Kevin Plank played football for the University of Maryland and noticed that while his compression shorts wicked away sweat and moisture, his cotton shirts had to be changed after every practice—which, in a cold place like Maryland is annoying. Plank gave prototypes to his teammates and perfected a synthetic-fibered shirt that kept players cool and dry. Plank created moisture-wicking apparel before leading brands such as Nike, Adidas, and Reebok, and the company quickly gained a devout following.

In recent years, Under Armour has become a champion of the underdog, as if emphasizing its grassroots beginnings. One ad shows ballerina Misty Copeland dancing en pointe while her rejection letter from a ballet academy is read. The letter says she has the "wrong body" for ballet. Now a soloist for the American Ballet Theater, she is an excellent spokesperson for the brand's messaging: "I will what I want," "will trumps fate," and "empowering active lifestyles." Under Armour is increasingly turning its attention to sports traditionally practiced by women, who are 47 percent of their consumer base. When the brand received flak for signing supermodel Gisele Bündchen as a spokesperson, they released a video of her roundhouse kicking a punching bag back dropped by mean-spirited messages sourced from Twitter.

While brands such as Lululemon misstepped and alienated female consumers when its founder was quoted as saying not every woman's body was made for yoga pants, Under Armour has a totally different approach. Under Armour aims to empower women to defy what others say or think about their bodies by shining a spotlight on athletes such as Copeland, or challenging people to redefine the work of a model or the training of a gymnast. In this way, Under Armour is purposely maintaining a mind-set of staying small: targeting lesser-tapped markets in order to fight off the idea that they are a big, faceless, monolithic company—in much the same way that Nike has separate branches for basketball, running, soccer, and the like. It also cultivates fanatic-user bases within these more niche communities, even though the company is now public and no longer a craft brand.

In recent years, Under Armour has invested over $700 million in technology, acquiring digital apps MapMyFitness, MyFitnessPal, and Endomondo. The future of Under Armour is a technology-enabled one, moving toward digital. At the heart of these acquisitions is really the company's community. Through these apps, the company is able to acquire fanatic-user bases of joggers, runners, health and wellness folks who may not yet have been integrated into the Under Armour world. They've acquired millions of users all over the world who can provide more data and insight into what this user base wants based on what they're doing and what products they're buying. At the SXSW 2016 Film, Media, and Music Festival, on the heels of Nike announcing the shuttering of the Nike Fuel Band, Kevin Plank announced that Under Armour was acquiring one million new members every eight days. Under Armour aims to sell more by enhancing existing and future products based off that data, thereby giving consumers more of what they're looking for. This is a great example of the ways you can grow when you take an existing fanatic-user base that is already passionate about something and invite others into the fold.

Not all brands have the resources and capability to acquire their own user base, which is why Hubba makes it really easy for retailers to view up-to-date product information from brands such as Under Armour and SKLZ. We now have more than fifteen thousand companies on our platform, each of which has their own unique stories.

We launched the Hubba Discovery Network early in 2016 to help brands showcase their products and their stories and to help retailers find thousands of exciting, innovative vendors that they may have never heard of before.

While in Los Angeles for Hubba's Discovery Network launch event, we showcased a great brand, Superfit Hero. Micki Krimmel raised $55,000 on Kickstarter to launch Superfit Hero, a woman's athletic apparel brand that is body-positive and size-inclusive, running from size 00 to 3XL. Quite simply, she was tired of everybody defining fit as super small or tiny for women. Athletic gear only goes up to a size twelve for women, yet the average size in the United States is a fourteen. That simple barrier of not being able to find athletic apparel in a size that fits can keep many women from working out altogether, as they become totally turned off from the very idea of stepping foot inside a gym. Krimmel set out to empower other women to wear apparel of high quality and high performance—wearing something in the gym that they can feel good about. Superfit Hero targets a fanatic-user base of health and wellness focused on women who may not fit the mold predetermined by most athletic apparel companies.

Krimmel knew from her experience as a roller derby player that athletic women come in all shapes and sizes. A fanatic-user base of roller derby and rugby players helped grow the brand's following and made it one of the most successful Kickstarter campaigns in the site's history.

Similarly, on the tech side of things, an app called PumpUp has become extremely popular. It's almost like Instagram for working out: keep track of workouts and health goals, while receiving positive feedback from a like-minded community. You can track your progress, post pictures of meals and workouts, and take part in new workouts posted by the community. While PumpUp is not necessarily a craft brand, it is a great example of how people are exploiting the passion and world of health. Another example of fanatic-user bases often occurs with new parents: people who want good-quality products for their child. In seeking out solutions to problems, they meet fanatic users of a certain product, which not only helps them solve a problem—such as reducing the waste caused by diapers, or finding organic baby toys—but also connects them to like-minded people. That initial fanatic-user base then becomes a community, where the consumer is not only connected to the product but also the people who helped them find it. Hopefully, in turn, they will help spread the word, thereby growing the brand and cultivating an army of people who believe in it.

It's not always enough to have a great product. Although World of Angus clearly spent a lot of time perfecting its dog shampoo, the company also ensured that is was creating something different—a world, if you will, where dog owners can engage with one another and dogs can get the things they need. In the same way, Superfit Hero and PumpUp are creating these worlds for health and fitness advocates to thrive. Micki Krimmel was able to connect with her fellow female athletes to create something specifically for women, while Kevin Plank relied on his teammates to give him feedback on early prototypes of moisture-wicking shirts. Because Jeremy Potvin himself was passionate about finding good-quality, made-in-

Canada goods for his dog, he was able to connect with like-minded individuals—both potential consumers and brands with which to collaborate—and grow that initial advocacy of fanatic users into a community.

ASSEMBLING LEAN MANUFACTURING

Just a few years ago, creating a tech company was really capital intensive. Historically, to start a company you needed everyone on site to collaborate, work together, and design together. All of the intellectual property and code needed to be secured within the walls of the actual company itself. You needed an office, a physical location. You needed to invest in the infrastructure and hardware—namely, servers to store and run the code. Infrastructure was generally the biggest, most capital-intensive aspect. Not only would you need a bunch of servers for the production environment, but you'd need to replicate and copy that across testing and development environments.

As if that weren't costly enough, if the app or site received more traffic, the company needed more horsepower in the form of more servers. Once you reached your processing limit, you would need more servers, and ordering the servers meant you would need a lead time to get them delivered to the company. God help you if the *Wall Street Journal* wrote an article, people logged in en masse, and your traffic spiked. Your overloaded system would likely crash. In the old world, there was no time to react and bring things up to speed.

That was then, when start-ups needed millions of dollars to get a product off the ground: buy servers, hire an IT person just for the servers, equip the company with power surge protectors, encryption software, and adequate heating and cooling systems to keep the servers happy. The necessary infrastructure was often cost prohibitive.

Then the notion of the cloud and cloud computing became more prevalent. The biggest change was distributed computing, most notably through service providers such as Amazon Web Services, commonly referred to as AWS. That division of Amazon made the initial huge capital outlay for servers and server farms, creating its own physical space with tons of computing power and all the infrastructure anyone could need in multiple locations, staffed by the right people. This allowed start-ups and developers to simply rent or lease, thereby storing and processing everything on Amazon's servers. And since AWS handles all the computing, if you receive more web traffic and need to flex up, you can easily do that. If you need less, AWS flexes it down a bit. It used to require thousands of dollars for a new server and lead time to get it to your location, but now you can rent out little pieces of computing and storage capacity here and there and receive a bill based on your actual usage at the end of the month. It has now become an ongoing operating expense, as opposed to a sizable upfront capital expense.

Instead of having to build the infrastructure, hire a team, and have everyone in a physical location, providers like AWS allows craft brands in the tech industry to focus on other things. The Amazons of the world undertook the investment in the climate control systems, the disaster recovery systems, the security systems, the staff, and the hardware so that you can be anywhere in the world with a small team, plug into Amazon's back-end infrastructure, and work from anywhere. Because of this, we have seen a massive proliferation of app and software companies emerge since 2008. The cost to establish a tech company has dropped from millions to hundreds of thousands. Almost everyone now builds off the Amazon infrastructure or something similar. AWS, which was launched in 2006, brought about the next generation of software companies that made the switch in 2007. After just ten years of operation, AWS reached $8 billion in revenue in 2015 and is predicted to hit $16 billion by 2017.

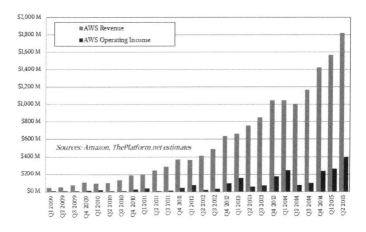

It used to be prohibitively expensive to establish a physical location, hardware, and infrastructure, but all of a sudden we're seeing people start their businesses from anywhere and everywhere, leading to tremendous innovation. There are also better teleconferencing and communication tools to aide this. All of the software code that used to have to be maintained within a tech company's own four walls is now stored in a cloud repository, GitHub, which almost every developer uses. You don't need to keep your software on premises anymore, as you can automatically merge pieces of code developed anywhere in the world. You don't need the servers or the security, and all of the computing power is done through a monthly rental bill as opposed to a huge capital cost. You can scale up and scale down as needed to do exactly what you need at a moment's notice. We now have faster servers, better security, and better infrastructure than anyone starting up a company just a decade ago could have ever dreamed of.

Everyone is now so accustomed to operating in the cloud that even when Hubba built its own infrastructure to host data for customers that did not want it hosted by a third party in the cloud, absolutely no one took us up on it.

We've also witnessed the rise of companies such as Airbnb, Uber, Netflix, Hulu, Reddit, Foursquare, Pinterest, which all run off of outsourced cloud services. These are companies that were able to start quickly and cheaply and that might not have otherwise had the capital needed from day one. Instead of needing millions, you may only need a few thousand. Instead of having to start investing in order to launch a product line, companies such as Dollar Shave Club and Hampton Creek can economically release products first and then raise capital from investors.

So what does this shift in the tech world mean for craft brands? Well, they have a very similar opportunity through lean manufacturing.

Dapple Baby is a great example of a craft brand that started with a good idea that may have never gotten off the ground if it weren't for new technologies and lean manufacturing approaches. Two mothers who didn't really believe the organic, green, chemical-free labeling of most household supply companies created the company. The two moms, Tamar and Dana, discovered that regular dish soap left behind "synthetic fragrances and persistent odor, plus a film that never seemed to come off." Tamar and Dana carefully selected ingredients for their products. The founders of Dapple Baby formulated cleaning solutions specifically for baby messes that were organic and green. They saw an opportunity and a niche market that solved a problem no one else was tackling.

The company adopted the slogan "By moms, for moms." After coming up with the idea, they quickly worked with manufacturers to get their product developed, honed their branding and packaging, and launched it to the world. It has since spread like wildfire in an almost unbelievable way. One of the reasons for the company's success, aside from its fantastic products, was how quickly the owners were able to get the products to market at a significantly lower cost than most traditional brands and manufacturing.

In the old world, you needed to establish a plant or a lab, get the money to build a facility, grow or source all of the ingredients, and run through iterations of bottling and branding, all of which could cost tens of millions of dollars just to get a product out the door. With the rise of new manufacturing models, craft brands are able to get off the ground faster than ever, in ways that are cheaper and much easier for them. It is more viable than ever to quit your day job, design and build a brand and product, and utilize the outsourced world to start a product-based company you're passionate about.

Historically, to create a cosmetics company, you likely needed to build the plant to manufacture the products, recruit scientists to formulate the ingredients, source a massive amount of materials (it's hard to find wholesalers who provide small orders), and hire someone to come up with the branding and packaging. All that, plus you would then need to find a distributor, interested retailers, and create a sales and marketing team.

What may have cost tens of millions of dollars is now relatively cheap. Now, someone wanting to start a cosmetics line could find a third-party manufacturer in North America, South America, Asia, or wherever and say, "Here are the ingredients I want. Here is the product I want. Go manufacture an initial batch of a thousand units." You can even use multiple manufacturers and tell each of them the secret sauce and instruct them to make it. There's no longer just one option for manufacturing, and creating products is faster than ever, so brands can swiftly go through various testing phases before they launch.

World of Angus evaluated five manufacturers before they settled on the one that created the shampoo they were most excited about. And with third-party manufacturing, scaling up is easier than ever. For instance, ceramic artist Ariel Zimman of RELM Studios knows that if she ever receives a large order she can't possibly fill on her own, she can work with Mudshark Studios, a high-volume production studio in Portland, Oregon. That way, Zimman can focus on creating new products and filling custom orders for clients, rather than churning out thousands of stacking bowls on her own. Before, receiving a huge order would have meant ordering more clay, kilns, or even upgrading facilities. Now businesses can more easily scale up and down with the option of third-party manufacturing. They can get amazing products out the door in shorter time frames with less overhead costs and quickly respond to what the public wants and likes before getting another product out into the marketplace.

It's also now possible to source packaging from outsourced companies that specialize in that area, hire a freelancer for branding, and list the finished product on a Shopify website to sell directly to consumers. With the rise of social media, marketing and communications can be done for free. Launching a brand no longer takes years of research and development, and brands can exist on a shorter funding runway. All of this can be accomplished within a couple of weeks, with maybe a couple thousand dollars.

Big hard-goods manufacturers have done something similar for years. Ford doesn't create the carburetor, the gears, or the interior plastic for every single the company produces. It works with a bunch of auto parts manufacturers and assembles the items to create a Ford product. The model has proven to work, and it has worked on a massive scale, but it was previously almost impossible to do such a thing on a small scale.

Now, a company like Dapple Baby can manufacture and launch products faster than ever before, cheaper than ever before, without having to overproduce, waste resources, or make compromises on their ingredients. New technologies allow for Dapple Baby's products to be biodegradable, free of synthetic dyes, fragrances, parabens, phthalates, or sulfates. Like World of Angus, Dapple Baby has created nontoxic products that resonate with consumers and the people they care about. Instead of being preoccupied with building and owning a manufacturing plant, warehouse, or maintaining relationships with distributors and retailers, brands can focus solely on the things they care about—

such as providing excellent customer service—versus issues of production and supply.

DIFFERENTIATING THROUGH SERVICE

———

Iconic craft brand Canada Goose does not discount its products, maintaining the exact same price for all products across all sales channels. If you shop online for a Canada Goose winter jacket via CanadianIcons.ca, two things will happen: an announcement for free overnight shipping anywhere in Canada (even in a blizzard), and a chat box from an actual person with an actual name and photograph, who welcomes you with exclamation points, will appear with the message, "It's great to catch you at Canadian Icons! I am here to help you with any questions/ advice you may need assistance with!"

The first listing on their site is not for a product at all, but the Canada Goose parka history—the story. The "retailer" isn't even trying to sell you a jacket. The company is more interested in engaging with you with tales of the brand's history and establishing a connection with a real person to answer questions and offer advice. Manufactured and tested in Canada since 1957, the brand boasts clientele such as Canadian Arctic Rangers working in subzero temperatures, US National Science Foundation researchers in Antarctica, oil rig workers, and Arctic Air pilots. In 2007, the Canada Goose invited two traditional sewers from a native Canadian Inuit community to collaborate with them on a parka—adding features that were unique and functional to a life lead in darkness eight months of the year.

Canadian Icons CEO Aron Slipacoff has been quoted as saying, "To fully appreciate a Canada Goose parka, you need to see its connection to Canada's Arctic peoples, how Canada Goose works with Inuit elders on design, how the company gives back to these communities. You need a more complete picture of the uniquely Canadian connection to the product to really get the feel for what makes it iconic."

As he noted on Shopify's blog, Slipacoff's mission for his website was to create a unique experience for visitors to buy iconic Canadian items and "get a taste of Canadian history and culture." This includes one-of-a-kind paintings and Manitobah Mukluks, along with Canada Goose jackets—mixing past traditions and contemporary items on a platform that looks more like a museum than an e-commerce site.

"There is a trend now where people want to become more knowledgeable about what they consume and spend money on. The marriage of these ideas was how CanadianIcons.ca was born," Slipacoff said. And knowing that customer service can be a key aspect in someone's decision to buy something, they offer guaranteed ninety-minute delivery in Ottawa and next-day delivery anywhere else in Canada, no matter what the weather.

CanadianIcons.ca and Nordstrom, at first glance, may seem like similar websites and buying experiences. Nordstrom has a massive back-end infrastructure, does very well as a retailer, and consumers recognize the name.

However, big names such as Nordstrom, Neiman Marcus, or even Dick's Sporting Goods don't offer free overnight shipping all the time, especially in blizzards. There is often a lack of information about brands on the large retailer websites, and visitors have to scroll through or search hundreds or thousands of listings for the one thing they really want or need. There is also no human connection available on theses site—no one welcoming you and offering to help with advice or questions.

Canadian Icons may not have as many resources as larger companies, but they have a tightly honed, positive experience, with better service that really focuses on the customer. Instead of investing in infrastructure such as brick-and-mortar locations or fancy websites, they have a super streamlined buying experience that lists products and offers help. The company owns no inventory; everything is drop shipped, so they have no warehouse, no inventory, no outstanding exposure, and they don't have to account for the cost of that or the manufacturing. They are really just a portal, whereas other retailers invest in inventory, deal with pricing changes, and hire people to manage stock and warehouses.

The question is no longer, "How can a small company like Canadian Icons compete?," but "How can big companies compete with brands that literally pop up overnight, offer better experiences, better customer service, and better product selection?"

Big retailers need to adjust their perspective from doing transactions to creating customer experiences. Brick-and-mortar retailers will survive only if they modify themselves toward experience and fulfillment—giving the consumer the information they need to buy the product right then and there, rather than having to go somewhere else.

Unfortunately, many large retailers are now choosing to keep lower amounts of stock on their shelves, and when none are left, they offer customers free shipping to their home. While this certainly does cut down on inventory costs and keeps a retailer from dealing with inventory and pricing changes, it negates the whole experience of a consumer seeking out a retailer in order to fulfill a transaction. When I go into a store, I would like to, and even expect, to take something home, whereas my expectations with an online retailer such as CanadianIcons.ca is entirely different and totally exceeded. They have created a reputation built on quality products and excellent customer service.

It is easier than ever for upstart companies to break into existing supply chains, and retailers need to step it up with their infrastructure and experience. Retailers do have an advantage in that they deeply understand the supply chain. They should be able to say, "We can have it to your house in two hours." There are better ways to operate if you're already functioning on such a large scale, yet many retailers are resting on their laurels, wondering why they even need to compete. A thousand Canadian Icon-like brands could pop up tomorrow without hesitation thanks to improvement in technology, and all of those little guys combined could eat away a meaningful chunk of market share like small piranhas feasting on a hippopotamus.

One brand that's doing particularly well in the online marketplace, and is often cited in business cases, is online shoe and clothing retailer Zappos. They're now a well-known company, with a reputation for their focus on the "wow factor." That means they will do whatever it takes to deliver an experience where a customer says "wow." The very core of that is providing great customer service, which means heavily investing in individuals who are great at that. Another component of their strategy is equipping customer service representatives with a budget so they can send gifts to customers. Maybe someone was having a bad day, or it's their birthday, or they had a negative experience. The representative not only has the authority, but the discretionary budget, to send flowers, cookies, and gifts to customers.

In general, there are three fundamental things consumers tend to care about: experience, price, and convenience. Canadian Icons nails the experience side of things by curating their site like a museum, providing great information, and exuding passion, while also adding on the convenience aspect with fast shipping. Zappos also provides good customer service and started out because brick-and-mortar retail shoe shopping often proved inconvenient: stores might not have a certain size or color in stock, and the founders recognized in 1999 no online retailers were specializing in shoes. Zappos aims to combine memorable service with endless selection to win over consumer loyalty. The company was so successful that just ten years after its founding, Amazon acquired it for $1.2 billion.

DRIVING A MISSION

———

Most people are familiar with Lululemon for both their clothing and their mission, which a fanatic-user base that grew into a sizable community embraced and spread. This helped the company catch on and become a mainstream brand. The company capitalized on the yoga craze, offering free classes at their stores and focusing on living healthy. Their mission was health and wellness. The company's very distinct shopping bags were imprinted with things like "Friends are more important than money." When you purchased a Lululemon product, you were not just buying spandex; you were buying into a philosophy, an ethos, a lifestyle, and an ideal.

Initially, their primary advocate group was composed of women. I remember receiving a Lululemon sweatshirt as a gift, and I admit I first thought it was weird, because at that time, Lululemon seemed to be a woman-centered clothing line. After some time, the advocate group that catalyzed around this one mission started to seep out, breaking through the ceiling and into the mainstream. In no time at all, everyone seemed to be wearing Lululemon and not just to the yoga studio or gym. In reality, it really didn't occur that suddenly. The company's tremendous success developed from a carefully crafted mission, story, and vision, coupled with a reliance on a core set of fanatic users who developed into a community that continued to grow.

When Lululemon started, they were up against mega brands such as Nike. Well-established, Nike is a mission-driven company as well, which interestingly also started with a core group. What happens when a brand like Nike grows to be a monolithic size? It has to cater to a larger audience, which can be much harder. Successful companies such as Nike that have become so broad have developed strategies to keep the company looking and feeling like a craft brand buy incorporating smaller offshoots that keep their missions more singular—for example, Nike Basketball or Nike Running. Both are very different worlds and a way for a big company such as Nike to tighten or hone its messaging to a wider range of consumers.

Lululemon was the new, young upstart. Customers believed and supported the company, and, in many ways, they were proud ambassadors of its mission. With success and a loyal following comes tremendous responsibility to not only maintain but also reinforce a brand's mission. As fanatic as customers may be about your brand and your products, the backlash can be massive if you deviate. If you're promoting health, wellness, and empowerment, you should probably not tell women (or imply) that most of them should not be wearing the company's yoga pants because they're not for overweight people. Chip Wilson, Lululemon's founder, stated in a 2013 TV interview, "Quite frankly, some women's bodies just don't actually work" for his yoga pants. Not surprisingly, he was forced to step down as chief innovation and branding officer of the company just a few weeks later. Wilson's comments were made in response to complaints the company had been receiving that its new line of yoga pants were sheer and you could see through them. The sheerness was not by design, and it subsequently became clear that the company had been skimping on materials to save costs. The public relations debacle severely damaged the company, and everyone was aware that the signature product was lacking in quality. The company had deviated from its mission and subsequently humiliated the women they were supposed to be empowering. Nike faced a similar backlash when reports of sweatshop labor in Indonesia surfaced. However, when a brand like Lululemon faces this kind of controversy, it isn't able to weather it as well. Nike, at the time, seemed big enough to be able to recover. With a passionate, mission-based brand like Lululemon, the slightest deviation triggers a huge drop in loyalty.

Recently, the family that founded Lululemon launched Kit and Ace, a luxury apparel brand that uses "technical cashmere" in clothing. Its mission is about quality and style—not at all like Lululemon's focus on health and empowerment. They're not out to make the world a better place, and they are feature-driven rather than community-driven. If they were to say, "Our clothes aren't for everyone, they're for a particular man or woman," it would probably not be a huge controversy.

Most companies whose success mimics this pattern have a mission-driven culture, especially in the craft world. That mission goes far beyond "sell more product, generate more revenue." On top of the pyramid is the mission, and everything else is a consequence, or subsequent to believing in that mission. Lululemon was not selling yoga pants—they were selling health, wellness, and empowerment. This might make you want to do yoga, in which case you're going to need yoga pants, which they can provide you with. Lululemon, and brands like it, project their passion to consumers, who in turn respond.

Likewise, Whole Foods Market is selling a lifestyle. The grocery chain has a clearly defined purpose that allowed them to start off small and grow pretty quickly. They wrapped their branding and execution around their purpose to promote health and the community. It's amazing to think that when you buy into that, you often don't mind that the prices are generally much higher than other stores (the company has even been investigated and fined for overcharging customers). Clearly, though, people are responding to the Whole Foods ethos, as the company is worth over $10 billion.

The mission is what penetrates the soul of people. There is something to connect with that resonates with consumers. It's definitely not the spandex itself, but the mission. It gives people a sense of purpose, which one desires when buying a product. Stories and missions justify a consumer's decision to purchase a quality product. It also activates an army of like-minded individuals who feel as if they are a part of something—like we're all in this together—thereby building a community.

Every one of the brands mentioned thus far in this book has one thing in common: driving a mission. Zappos started with the aim of having the widest selection of shoes, the best customer service, and always focusing on the "wow factor." Hampton Creek is addressing issues in the food supply chain by coming up with plant-based alternatives to eggs. World of Angus curates well-made products for dogs to promote healthy pet lifestyles and reignite Canadian manufacturing. Dapple Baby provides nontoxic cleaning solutions for every day messes unique to toddlers and kids. Crane Humidifiers brings style and health together using great design. Canada Goose creates seriously stylish and functional winter parkas that are made in Canada and delivered with great customer service. GoPro promotes living your life, sharing it, and connecting with others. SKLZ is committed to a healthy lifestyle through training athletes with the company's equipment. Dollar Shave Club is making men's grooming a breeze, hassle-free, and accessible, with the ultimate aim of owning the bathroom.

Just over a year ago, a talk I gave at a tech event was recorded. "The Lies We Tell Ourselves" focused on what entrepreneurs say to each other and themselves, as well as the advice they give to others. One of the biggest misnomers around is "Do what you love." Most people think this is great advice. I don't necessarily think so. You can love many things, but if the market isn't big enough, it doesn't matter how good you are or how passionate you are. What I used to always say is I don't necessarily aspire to sell more Nikes to Walmart, but what I love doing is creating big, important companies—monster companies. That's what I discovered I loved. Launching Hubba to allow brands and retailers to connect and correct product and brand misinformation seemed like an amazing and fertile area for us to build a monster company.

When I met Crane Humidifiers, all of that changed. I went from waking up in the morning thinking about nothing but creating a big, important company, to realizing that what I really loved was championing these amazing craft brands—the ones with a mission and a passion. It doesn't matter if it's a product from a large multinational, such as Starbucks coffee, or from a small cart such as Ole Latte. It runs right down the chain to people who have just started and are creating great stories.

I'm the guy who feels like he "saw the light" and now

wakes up every morning asking how we can shine a spotlight and make these brands visible to the rest of the world. Although I believed Hubba was a purpose-driven company at the outset, I now see that our purpose has evolved to helping brands reach the right people.

This is why we launched the Hubba Discovery Network. Hubba is generally for retail buyers and influencers to find the world's most interesting brands and products. With the Discovery Network, we're allowing thousands of brands the visibility and notoriety they might not otherwise have with retail buyers.

With the Discovery Network, retailers can diversify from the few incumbent brands they typically carry and differentiate with thousands of new and exciting products. This democratizes the process for brands, providing an equal playing field for the big and little players. It also means connecting with people and brands on the platform, thereby providing for community and collaborative partnerships.

Industry trade shows are the old world of visibility and are often super expensive and inconvenient to travel to and exhibit at: having to ship your product, book flights and accommodations, set up and tear down a booth, and all without any guaranteed results. It's bizarre to think that in today's world of new technologies and increasing connectivity you still have to physically go to a trade show to discover new products. Hubba is a 24/7 trade show that is always fresh and tailored to you. Building a big company is exciting, but building one that helps so many amazing brands and retailers is extremely rewarding.

CONCLUSION

Many of the craft brands mentioned in the book all took similar approaches. The ones who were and are successful are the ones who started off small as niche markets to establish a really solid foundation that set the stage before they launched into orbit like a rocket into the mainstream market. The ones that perform the best are focused, starting small before they go big. The ones that aim too big, too broad, and too wide don't seem to get into orbit.

Macroeconomic conditions—including the new focus on value and resonance—and the stage that's set—in terms of distribution, different pricing models, technology and decentralization—means that the future is very bright for craft brands. The genie has been let out of the bottle and it's not going back. In fact, there are going to be more and more of these different formulas and varieties of commerce as we move forward. As that starts to happen, it will permit an even greater number of craft brands to enter the market.

What's small is going to be huge. Craft brands have the ability to take more and more of this world. This is not a trend that will reverse, even if we thought it could. It can't. If anything it's likely to accelerate in the future. Whoever takes it seriously—takes advantage of these opportunities in decentralization and the like—will win. The ones who are successful will quickly recognize and exploit technological breakthroughs in distribution and manufacturing and act on them. The ones who are successful will not only innovate, they will continue to innovate and not rest on their laurels.

This is also the best time to be a consumer. Retailers can succeed if they alter their practices, but as a consumer, you have the advantage of choice and quality. We're exposed to more things. We have information available to us all the time versus having to work to find it. And now that there are more brands popping up using third-party manufacturing or other new technologies, they are able to focus on creating the best possible product, rather than advertisements and sales or issues of supply. Smaller brands generally produce higher-quality products for consumers, and we now have access to some of the best-made goods. Not only that, but craft brands are addressing our needs with better-experience stores that resonate, communities that make us feel valuable, and missions that we believe in—all in ways that big brands cannot execute as easily.

At the end of the day, commerce is very simple: I am a consumer who has a problem and needs a solution. If I have to hang a painting, I'll need a hammer and nails. Commerce is just the fulfillment of those needs. As consumers, we have more exposure to things that can solve our problems. Instead of twenty options available, we now have access to two hundred. Not only that, but the top-two options that are the best for me bubble up to the surface because the data and information are there. That's a pretty amazing place for a consumer.

What you can learn from the stories of successful craft brands is to start small before you go big. The whole belief system underlying the martial arts practice Krav Maga is that most fights only last fifteen seconds. That's all. You're obviously going to do everything you can in those fifteen seconds to make sure that you win. Whether it's using a fire extinguisher or it's biting, it doesn't matter. Forget the beautiful science of boxing, or the amazing Tae Kwon Do skills you have perfected over the years. It's about winning those fifteen seconds, and that's it.

This is a battle. This isn't about being pretty and a perfect MBA case study. It's about using everything available to you right now to be able to take your mission, vision, and products to the mainstream world. It's all there for the taking. Before, you used to be locked in one room with nothing around you. Now, there are amazing tools and instruments at your disposal in order for you to fight and win.

APPENDIX

TEN BREAKOUT CRAFT BRANDS - 2016 EDITION

LAZY JACK PRESS

Lazy Jack Press creates beautiful bow ties, pocket squares, and socks. That may not seem so amazing, as there are a lot of companies that do. But what makes Lazy Jack Press so unique and amazing is that it's not about *what* they are making, but *who* they are making it for. They manufacture ultra-high-quality products using the same twenty-one momme silk as Hermes and featuring standout designs such as Red Solo Cups, Beer Kegs, Fried Eggs, and, of course, the Mullet—business in the front, party in the back. Lazy Jack Press makes beautiful quality accessories for people who never forget to play as hard as they work.

www.lazyjackpress.com

THING INDUSTRIES

Bridie Picot and Matt Smith are the sharp minds behind homeware brand Thing Industries. Mentioning the people behind the brand first is crucial, as Thing Industries is infused with their distinct personalities. At first glance, their products seem like chairs and rugs, but the longer you view them, the more you realize they are functional art. The Sacrificial Chair, Brick Blanket, Beast Blanket, and the Indoor Stoop are just a few items that will make your home a lot more interesting. They are conversation starters that are sure to leave your guests with little pangs of envy.

www.thingindustires.com

WHISKEY INK & LACE

WHISKEY, INK, & LACE

Whiskey, Ink, & Lace are self-described as "a collection of bath and body goods with rustic americana flair that will treat your everyday life to a li'l handcrafted lovin'." Still, this doesn't capture how amazing the brand is. Whiskey, Ink, & Lace currently offers over two hundred products, all made in Seattle, using natural, sustainably sourced ingredients. No harmful chemicals, vegan- and cruelty-free, and luxurious—not to mention clever: their products include Viking Beard Balm, Pirate Aftershave, Lumberjack Matte Pomade, and the Duke Stache Wax.

www.whiskeyinkandlace.com

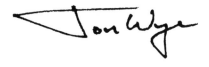

JON WYE

When someone asks you how you got the idea to start your company and the answer starts with, "And then I met a girl," you know whatever comes next is going to be great. In Jon Wye's case, he found that he was passionate about crafting belts and leather goods after he made a belt buckle on a creative first date. Fast-forward twelve years, add some very clever marketing, and a product that bests the competition, and Jon Wye is the king of independent handmade belt-makers. All items are still made by Jon's own hands in his Washington, DC-based workshop.

www.jonwye.com

SURF-FUR

When you meet while surfing, get married, and come up with the idea for a business all on the same beach, it's safe to say being at the beach is pretty important to you. Such is the story of Cynthia and Zenon Issel, founders of Surf-fur, the world's leading innovator, creator, and producer of high-quality, high-performance clothing for water lovers. Designed to help people of all ages stay warmer, perform longer, and feel better while following one's passion—whether it's surfing, kayaking, or anything related to waves and water. Product aside, what also makes Surf-fur amazing is its vast network of passionate ambassadors championing their wares wherever they go.

www.surf-fur.com

CHROME INDUSTRIES

Two decades ago, armed with a sewing machine and a handful of military-grade truck tarpaulin, Chrome Industries started a quest to design the toughest messenger backs on the market. The colors, fabrics, and, of course, the trademark seatbelt bucket make a Chrome bag distinct. More than just visually appealing, Chrome's wares are street tested, meaning they are often a bicyclist's first choice. These bags provide protection from the elements while still looking sleek (not like you just repelled down from the mountains).

www.chromeindustries.com

SUPERFIT HERO

Micki Krimmel, founder of Superfit Hero, is leading the charge in the body-positivity movement. As a competitive roller derby player, Krimmel knows that women and athletes come in all shapes and sizes, but their exercise gear does not. The fitness industry largely ignores women larger than a size twelve, yet the average size in the USA is a fourteen. Superfit Hero is the first fitness clothing brand to offer high-quality performance ware in sizes XS to 3XL. Because athletes come in all sizes.

www.superfithero.com

PHIN & PHEBES

Pronounced "Fin and Feebes," this premium ice cream brand resides deep in the heart of Brooklyn, New York. With flavors such as Banana Whama, Coconut Key Lime, Ginger Cookie Snap, and Vanilla Cinnamon, Phin and Phebes as made a name for itself—not only with catchy, memorable names but also by not adding stabilizers or syrups. The result is ice cream with all-natural ingredients, originating in the founding belief that ice cream can be one of the purest foods, if made properly. Hormone-free dairy is sourced from family-owned farms across New York, Rhode Island, and Massachusetts—ensuring the importance of all-natural farms.

www.phinandphebes.com

LUMENUS

Being seen is important for a lot of things in life, but it's absolutely vital when it comes to cyclist safety. Traditionally, the solution was bright colors and reflectors, but that doesn't always go far enough anymore. Thus the Lumenus jacket was developed, and the company focused on creating attractive safety clothing with built-in LED lights—allowing cyclists to be seen at any time of day. The true technology is not the lights, but that the clothing connects to a smartphone via Bluetooth. This way, phones connect to mapping apps and allow the jacket to communicate when you are breaking and turning. Genius in action.

www.lumenus.com

GILSON SNOWBOARDS

Gilson Snowboards is an artisan snowboarding company that designs boards from locally sourced wood, grown in central Pennsylvania. Their close-knit team of designers, craftsmen, and adventurers merge Pennsylvania woodworking heritage with the precision of modern technology—producing snowboards of the highest quality and construction. Perhaps the most interesting part of the Gilson story is the Snowboard Farm: legend has it, there are fifteen trees and a patch of grass between where the CEO lives and the shop where the boards are made. Thus they eat, sleep, and breathe snowboards. The new board you unwrap has never been any place other than the farm.

www.gilsonboards.com

ABOUT THE AUTHOR

———

 BEN ZIFKIN has spent the last fifteen years helping some of the world's largest organizations leverage technology to compete in business. After living and working in North America, Europe, and Asia, he has become a trusted advisor to senior executives of Fortune 1000 companies.

A repeat founder, Ben has built three organizations with successful exits and raised significant venture funding. His companies have been recognized as Top 3 Best New Start-Ups, Top 20 Most Innovative Companies, Fast 50 Companies to Watch, and Hot 50 Fastest Growing Companies.

His most recent business, Hubba, is the fastest growing business-to-business network connecting brands and retailers. Through this network, Hubba is building out the world's richest, most comprehensive data set of product information. Hubba is routinely recognized as one of the most powerful companies powering the next generation of commerce. Utilizing years of experience dealing with large organizations, Ben has focused his effort to shining a spotlight on amazing craft brands and their products.

Ben is heavily involved with the technology community and sits on the board of directors of Ladies Learning Code, an organization focused on increasing the digital literacy of women, and the Upside Foundation, a charity that works with start-ups to donate 1 percent of their equity in support of local communities. In addition, Ben advises HackerYou and Toronto's MaRS Discovery District, and he mentors at the Next 36 and Founder's Institute.

A proud Canadian, Ben makes his home in Toronto with his wife and two children.

Made in the USA
Charleston, SC
16 June 2016